Your Conscious Brain/Mind

Gary Deines

Amazon Publishing

First published in 2023

Copyright © Gary Deines

All rights reserved.

No part of this publication may be reproduced, stored or transmitted in any form by any means, electronic, mechanical, photocopying or otherwise, without the prior written permission of the authors.

Read to children, they fall asleep. Read by an adult, they wake up. We are all "babies" when it comes to Cognitive Science. That's what makes this book a MUST read for all human beings. Bit by bit, I got it.
-- Sara Taylor, Amazon Publishing Pro's

Dedication

This book is written for and dedicated to all the human beings on earth. We collectively make our future a Heaven or Hell. We, the quality of our thinking, cause life or death, now and forever.

This book is dedicated to thinking. Its purpose is to improve the quality of thought for us all.

You choose who you are becoming. These mental techniques are designed to help you be you.

Classical mechanics is to Quantum mechanics

what Quantum mechanics is to Conscious mechanics.

If you know how your Conscious brain/mind works and how it logically co-relates important symbols, then you can directly make it work better for your lifetime. You can program you!

Table of Contents

Dedication 3
Preface 5
What is Cognitive Science 8
    Introduction 8
    Conscious Brain/Mind (CBM) 10
    How to Use this Book .... **Error! Bookmark not defined.**
    Brain Is the Hardware 12
    Neuron Cells 13
    Mind Is the Software 14
    Defining Consciousness 15
    Life Is the Overall Point 15
    Boutons are Civilized 16
    Boutons are Moral 18
    Consciousness Is Conducted 18
    Your Career Manifest Destiny 20
    HDSA Opportunity 21
    Hierarchy 22
    Dimensionality 23
    Seriality 24
    Alternatives 25
    Dikw Symbolism 26
    Homework Assignment 27
    Partology… Think Again 28
    Truth Is Power 28
    Certified Metacognitions 30
    In Sum 30
Cognitive Engineering Examples 32
Glossary of Cognitive Science Terms 68
The Moral Part of Cognitive Science 87
About the Author 91

Preface

It is undoubtedly true that many stories have been told and a great many books written. They generally fall into one of two categories. The first is the oldest. Primarily fiction, it has evolved from myth and legend. It concerns human efforts to understand the world and communicate the origins of behavior and its consequences as lived through human experience and character. It is highly subjective, often philosophical in nature, and may be thought of as mapping an author's cognitive realm.

The second category of books is considerably more recent. It documents our struggle to understand physical reality in its many different forms. It concerns the human attempt to understand the contents and mechanics of the world, our place in it, and ourselves by experiment, observation, and quantification. In contrast to fiction, it claims objectivity, logic, and mathematics as its own.

As an academic computational neuroscientist, I lived in the second of these two worlds. However, over the years, I slowly became disenchanted with my studies in a realm that became increasingly magical.

Last year Professor Deines, one of the earliest practitioners of cognitive neuroscience, initiated an email correspondence with me about his theory concerning consciousness. It had reached a point where he thought it might be of great value to communicate to a wider audience. Initially, in our emails, there was indeed a clash of two cultures. The cognitive culture of Deines and my physiological culture of neuroscientific mechanisms.

Nevertheless, our interactions induced a transformational reconfiguration of how I was thinking. It required an understanding not of a brain consisting of an infinity of interacting physiological mechanisms but as an organ that, as it is actually experienced, is tightly integrated to form a whole from all its functional parts.

Specifically, I was clearer and became more focused on how I wanted to spend my time, with whom, and what the next-step output would be. I had become a little mentally discombobulated, working at cross purposes, and had lost that laser focus of youth. The HDSA/Dikw model of thought proposed by Deines and introduced in the following chapters provides cognitive training that refocused my life in a powerful way. There were less questions and more answers. Intentional clarity acted as a mental power. As I continue to become clearer, in both my logical and moral trains of thought, my life improves, and I get better.

This required no small effort on my part and revealed much of the dogma I had unknowingly absorbed during decades of academic neuroscience. Once freed, I have begun to recognize how many of my thoughts concerning brain function have taken on a new meaning and even new vigor. This has become one of his greatest gifts to me.

It is a rare book indeed that finds an author integrating the two cultures. The subjectivity of lived experience and the objective mechanics of cognition. This integration is generative and evolves as you come to terms with a model/procedure that emerges from cognition. However, to do this also requires a new language, or at least many new terms to describe the theory and develop your resultant mental model. Understanding this requires application, but the rewards, both subjectively and objectively, are unlimited. It is a reward that few books offer.

Allan D. Coop, Neuroscientist, Grenfell, NSW, Australia

What is Cognitive Science?

Cognitive Science is a new science having been birthed in England in the Nineteen-seventies. It is an eclectic science in that it studies all that the human mind has produced in order to better understand the body organ called a Conscious brain/mind (CBM). By seeing what the CBM has produced, we can back into how it works. You know the tree by the fruit that it bears.

Why do this? Why study the CBM in humans? Simple, if you know how it works then each person can take intended, ideological action to make theirs work better. That is good for us all.

This insight has profound economic and moral impact upon any civilization. Keep in mind, the human mind is the most valuable, expensive, and underutilized resource in the world today. By some estimates we scientists believe that the average utilization of the Conscious brain/mind is around 10%. That level of waste, wasting 90% of our potential mental skill, is unacceptable. We all need and can do much better. The ideas in the book have been designed to help.

Better understanding your Conscious brain/mind is accomplished via metacognition. This means you become skilled at thinking about how you think. To help do that, this book is organized into four sections, as follows:

1. First will explain cognition, and Cognitive Science, with 23 imaged points. Each point has a title, image, and brief description. They cover both the science and its practical use.

2. Next a number of "Examples" are illustrated to help explain how to use the 23 defined points. By then you should be able to personally use the knowledge provided herein. That's the start. Point by point; all people can understand how their CBM works. This is what makes you smarter. Note: We do not program you. You intentionally program you.

3. To support the 23 points, a Glossary is provided. If you do not understand a term, look it up in the glossary. All knowledge, both the knowledge in this book and what you have accumulated in your head, is ideally symbolized and can be named by a term or phrase.

4. Finally, the reader may choose three actions to get personal questions answered and to further their insights: (a) send homework and questions to GaryDeines@Boutonics.com and my people will respond, (b) signup for the www.CogSci101.com course (in a local class or online), and/or (c) apply for membership to www.Metacognitions.org. This is the association of professionally trained Cognitive Engineers that use the CMC Service mark. Enjoy the mental journey. It will be a very productive activity for Life. We're here to help. -G

How to Use this Book: In reality we know nothing, for the truth is in the depths. - Democritus

This book can be read to a child at night, in a monotone, to put them to sleep. Show the image and then read a page. Do this slowly. That quiets their mind. It's boring. The young child will fall asleep.

During this repetitive process of an adult reading this book to a child, the adult learns how their Conscious brain/mind works, bit by bit. The adult gets smarter.

This book is used in www.CogSci101.com. This is a Cognitive Science course being taught online, in High Schools, and at universities. Or, this book can be part of any CogSci course.

Companies also hold meetings on the ideas contained in this book. Personnel training, Quality Control, Sales, Marketing, and Leadership are all mindset functions.

The insights contained in this book are also relevant to Churches, Organizations, and Political processes. We all have a Conscious brain/mind that can be self-led to greater levels of performance. Idea improvement is found in group dialogue.

These ideas are universal. Bit-by-bit, each idea makes you smarter. That is the one purpose of this book.

NOTES:
As an adult, this is not a book you can skim read. Instead, you must think about each of the 23 points carefully. The knowledge contain herein is new, it's meta-knowledge; a metacognition.

As you read a point (each point is on one page), contemplate its meaning. Then say it in your own words. It is OK to use idea synonyms. Make comments on the Notes section in each page.

Then link the new point into all the previous points. In this way, as linked, the ideas contained herein will work their magic.

Babies

Children

People

Groups

"Thinking is the hardest work there is, which is probably the reason so few engage in it." - Henry Ford.

Introduction: How to become much smarter.

The Conscious brain/mind (CBM) is an organ that processes co-related symbols, called ideological memes (analogous to physical genes), as symbols carried upon energy waves.

It senses, acts, learns, and remembers; what to do, given a situation. It sees relevant external *content* always in an intentional Self *context*. It uses multiple simultaneous logics to do this.

CBMs are designed to help you live better, for longer, on less. They are all re-programmable.

If you learn the *metacognition* in this book, if you know how you think essentially, how self-evolved ideological memes control behaviors, then you can make your Conscious brain/mind work better for your and our lifetimes.

_____
_____
_____
_____
_____
_____

Why do you want to get smarter? What would that mean to your life quality?

Conscious Brain/Mind: It intentionally links data, information, knowledge, and wisdom.

Words matter intellectually. What we Cognitive Scientists have learned is that words (actually, all symbols, represented in all media) exist and mentally co-relate, creating useful insights, efficient behaviors, and life and/or death actions.

Take, for example, the word "metacognition." Meta (an ancient Greek philosophical term) means above, below, before, and after; it is the surrounding space. Cognition means thinking in cogs, in pieces. So, metacognition is the cognition that surrounds your cognition. It frames how you think.

In this book, you will learn metacognition that is based upon how both the Universe and a Conscious brain/mind work. It is called "**Partology**". It is based upon four overlapping logics (HDSA). It classifies symbols into Data, Information, Knowledge, and Wisdom (Dikw).

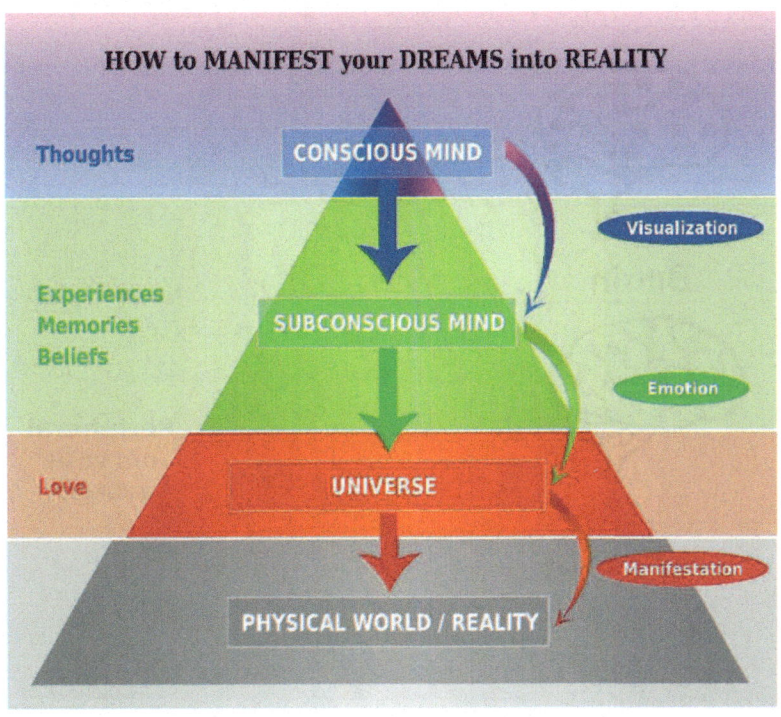

_____
_____
_____
_____
_____
_____

Accurate metacognition makes you smarter. All people should learn how they know.

Brain Is the Hardware: It is developed by the chromosome genes.

Brain is the neurons that are distributed into an **A**fferent (sensation in), **C**ognitive (decision making), and **E**fferent (instruction out) system.

This **ACE** pathway of neurons makes up the Central (CNS) and Peripheral Nervous Systems (PNS). This is the physical hardware. The CNS is for judging decisions, and the PNS is used for (1) sensation symbol input and (2) decided instruction output.

A Conscious brain/mind is an Input, Process, Output machine (IPO); that learns and remembers the best behaviors; given a situation intent. The brain is the physical hardware of this system.

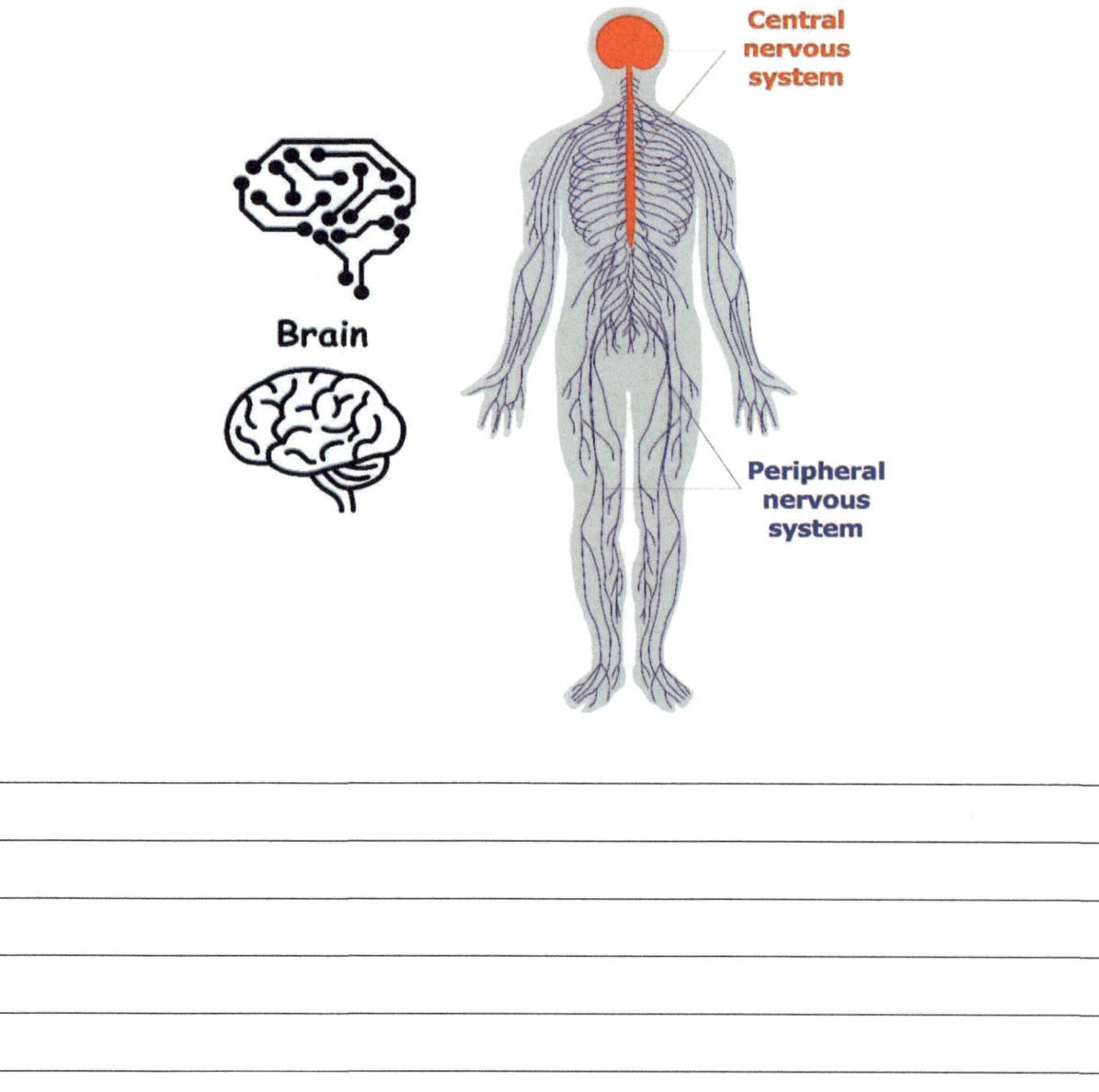

_____
_____
_____
_____
_____
_____

DNA develops and places neurons. This is the Conscious brain/mind hardware.

12 Your Conscious brain/mind

Neuron Cells: At birth, each person has approximately 80 billion neuron cells.

Neurons are DNA created-and-placed cells that collect, hold, and release electromagnetic energy; as quantized waves, creating insightful and meaningful symbols. At birth, they are not connected.

Neurons are ACE linked into a sense-in, decision-making, and instructions-out organic computer.

Neuron dendrites (roots) accept electrical input from the upstream neurons. Axons (branches) move that energy to other neuron locations. The energy jumps via the bouton (buds) in the synapse.

The sensation energy roots, branches, and buds pixelate your Conscious brain/mind into useful awareness; for your lifetime. They fire, creating symbols as meaningful content-in-context.

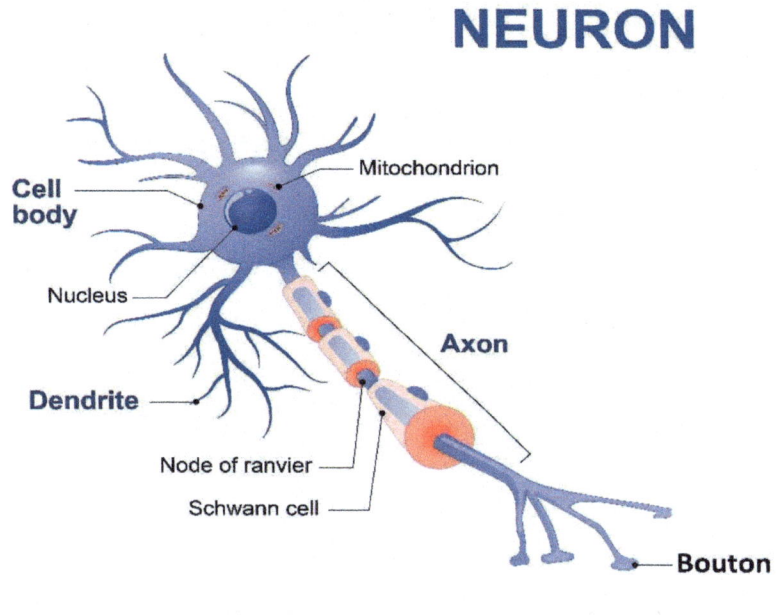

_____
_____
_____
_____
_____

The synaptic bouton is the mind pixel. They grow from use and connect up your neurons.

Mind is the Software: Each human can consciously reprogram themselves (to an extent).

Mind is the boutons that grow, based on repetitive usage, into a synapse, connecting neuron paths.

These boutons are mind pixels. They learn to fire together, creating symbolized content-in-context that is then viewed and reviewed by the Conscious brain/mind organ.

The brain is *physical* and the mind is *ideological*. The mind is the programmed <u>software</u> that runs on the brain neuron/bouton hardware; Self-selected for the creation of a particular person.

Mind consciously senses, learns, and remembers how the physical world works. It remembers what works and does not work, by a situation, for its more abundant lifetime. Self intentionally fulfills itself. Your Self creates yourself. You do this by what you choose to think, believe, and do.

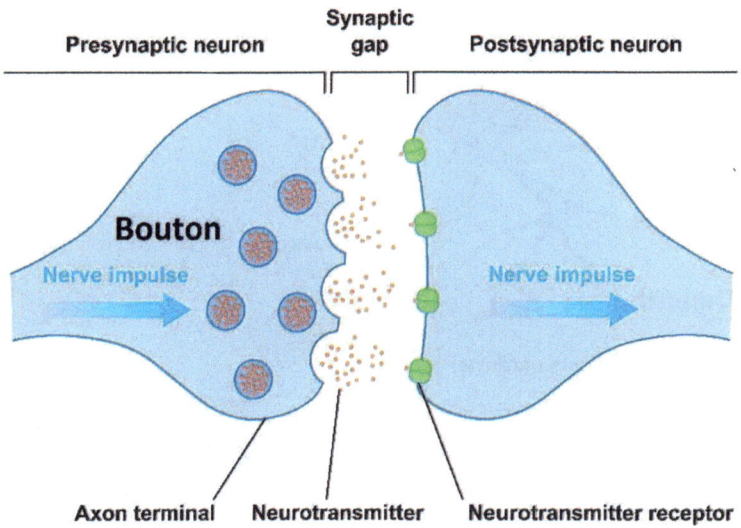

_____
_____
_____
_____
_____

A mindset is built bouton bit-by-bit . It is personally symbolic; an intended, created Self.

14 Your Conscious brain/mind

Consciousness is the Intent-ware: One idea is being intentionally aware of others.

Brain is physical. Mind memory is symbolized into correlated, ideological a/effectors. From the brain/mind layers, a *Conscious awareness* emerges in the meta-physical milieu. Meta means the above, below, before, and after space that surrounds the physical. It's the formed opportunity space, the foreknowledge for life-or-death behaviors.

Consciousness is the sixth sense. It is bouton's being subjectively aware of other boutons. How do we know this? Because boutons learn to fire together. In doing so, they co-relate experience.

Boutons that fire together keep firing together. This correlated process creates a sense> decide> act>, << feedback remembered consciousness; in memory. It is **a/effective**: a future-back affect and a past-forward effect, quantized at the same time.

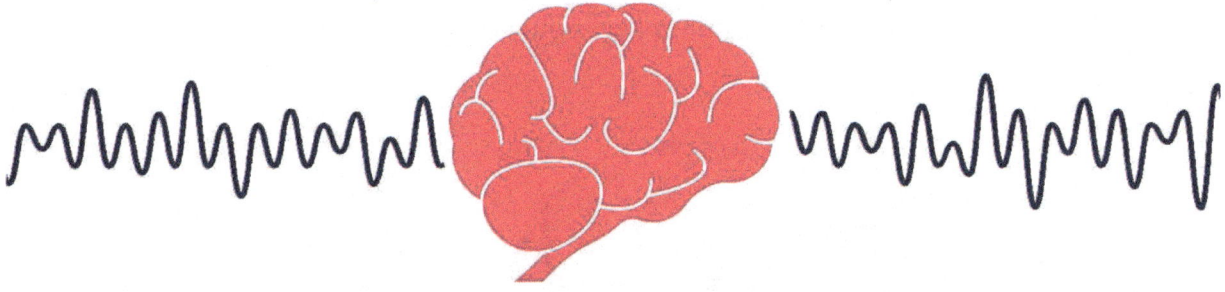

_____
_____
_____
_____
_____

Symbolic Input >> Cognition >> Behavior Output. If this (this & this), then do so and so.

15 Your Conscious brain/mind

Life Is the Overall Point: What can you, and we, now do to live better?

It is important to note that Life (living better on less for longer) is the metaphysical/physical context of consciousness. Living things create anew. They act to shelter themselves from the corrosive external forces by cocooning themselves in useful ideas and real physical structures.

The poet Bob Dylan stated, "Come in and I will give you shelter from the storm." The conscious hermit crab has gene-or-meme learned to take its soft body and place it into a leftover shell.

Why? These actions allow a thing to live better, for longer, on less. As Darwin once observed, the Universe promotes the more efficient and intelligent life forms. They have foreknowledge.

Why does a hermit crab find an unused shell to crawl into? They have learned doing that improves the quality and longevity of their life.

Same with humans. We learn to do the things that shelter us and comfort us; for our lifetimes.

_____
_____
_____
_____
_____

A good life, for all, can be built up. Add one good idea and its behavior at a time.

16 Your Conscious brain/mind

Boutons are Civilized: Both boutons and people are better together, in useful alignment.

No bouton is an island. They learn from each other via the collective firing and holding of all other boutons. This in-formed, group-waved synchronized firing creates a community pull.

Together boutons work better. This is why you must consciously think about it. The more you think about issues, subjects, situations, and opportunities; the smarter you will become.

The formula is b1 + b2 + b3 + etc. >> intelligence. >> is the causal sign. Consciousness is not =. By situation, based on intent, there is an ideal set of things to do, in a defined order, to efficiently achieve any life objective. Boutons symbolize that. They learn and remember what works best. The bouton bits; they symbolize behavioral intelligence which is good or bad for life.

It's called *Partology*. Boutons, those mind pixels, learn to team up intentionally for life.

_____
_____
_____
_____
_____

Many boutons make a symbol. Many symbols make a thought. Thoughts make a mind.

Boutons are Moral: Why care about others? It's for our lives.

Together, we are better for the life of us all. That is the *moral part* of the Conscious brain/mind.

Boutons, like humans, live via a/effect energy transactions. In the bouton case, they must process a certain quantity of neurotransmitters over time. Mental pathways, that foreknowledge, is built via attrition. Not used boutons kill neurons. Boutons must go along to get along.

At birth, we all have billions of neurons that are not needed, not used, and thereby die out. Your mental ideas are created and maintained in the boutons that are used and remain active. The idea created boutons that fire together, in a community, have a higher probability of staying alive. Bouton strength, and insightful human behavior, is formulated in this collective behavior.

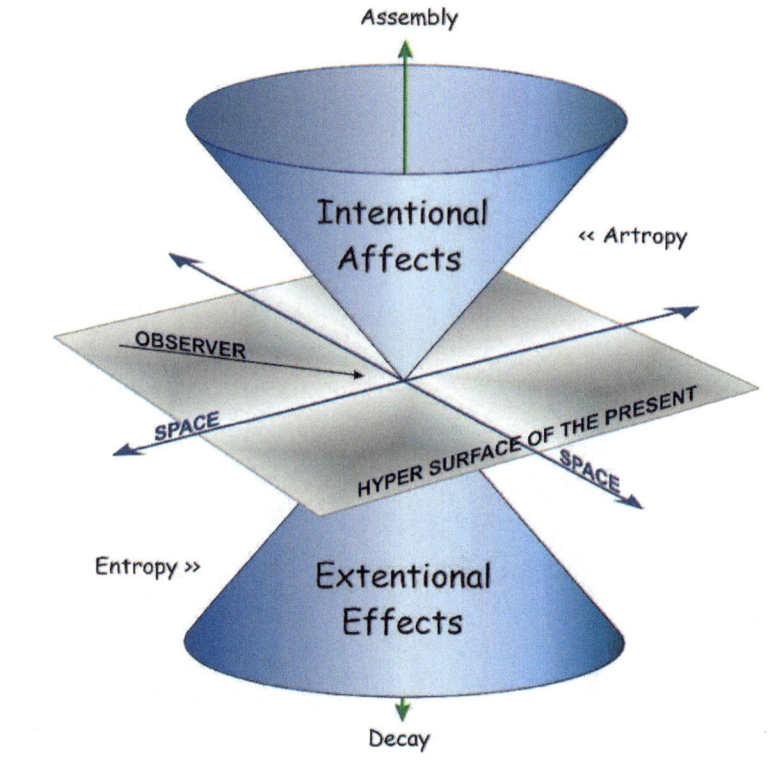

_____
_____
_____
_____
_____
_____

Assemble Life and decay Death. Do this step-by-step.

Consciousness is Conducted: Parts always affect the whole. Your part can be the assembly key.

In space, over time, all things are prior assembled and then will decay without maintenance; this is entropy. New things can be artfully constructed (artropy) and have a half-life; then, they will materially erode and decay.

One bouton is a vector. A collection of boutons is a tensor. Effects are past forward forces. Affects are future back opportunistic forces. All things are a/effected all the time.

Opportunity-for-life is a future-back phenomenon. It starts in the future, curving and structuring the opportunistic present. It is not deduced or induced; but consciously *conducted*, point by point, via affection. Conscious intentions change the physical world. We humans are in control.

That affective force is named artropy. The opportunity for life more abundant is the *invisible hand* that guides bouton co-relations. Boutons are sensitive to and practical for life.

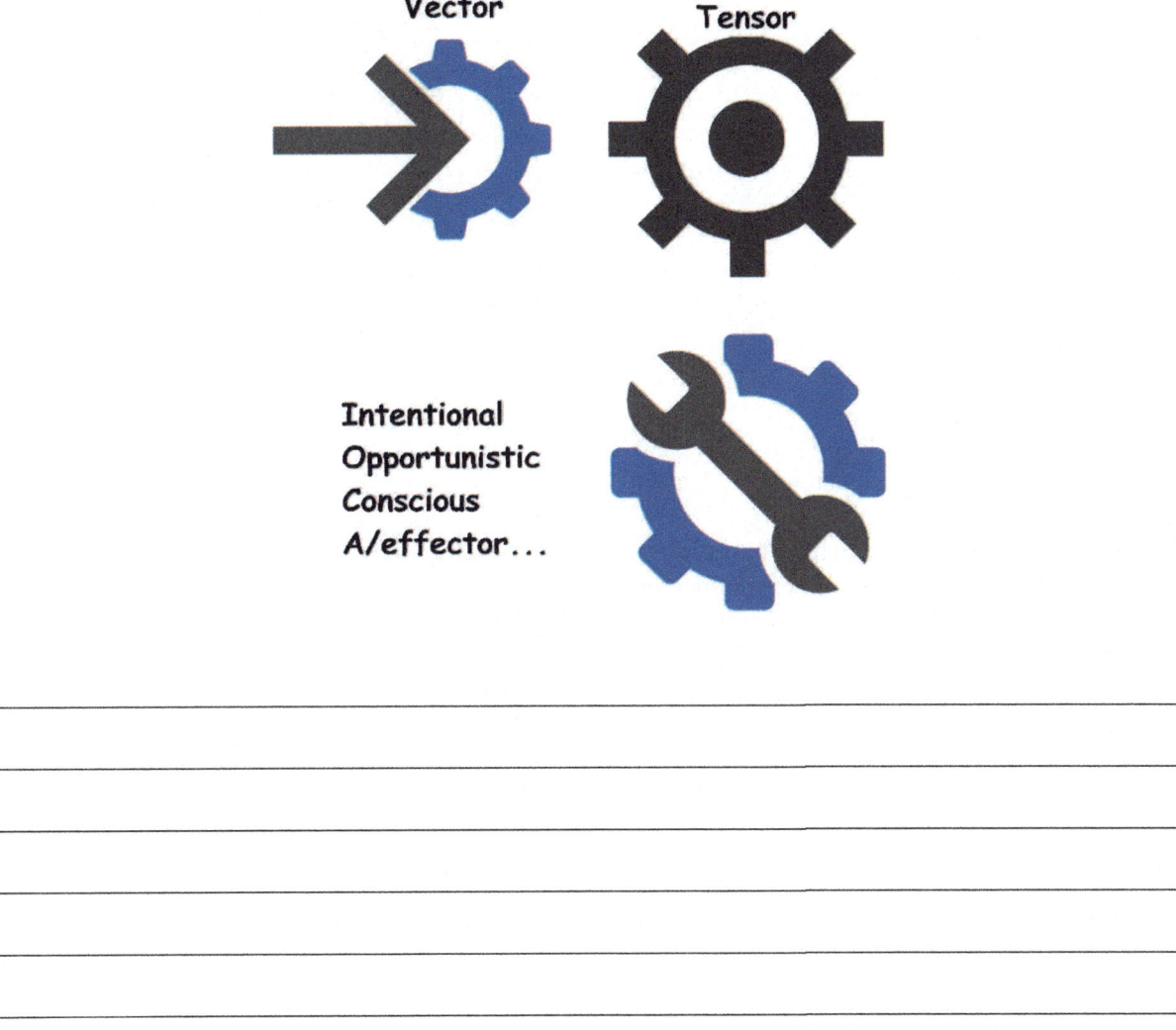

_____
_____
_____
_____
_____

Life opportunities naturally and consciously affect material structures.

19 Your Conscious brain/mind

Your Career Manifest Destiny: Do you know someone in their perfect job?

Each person has an idealized Career Manifest Destiny. This is the ideal, creative work you should be doing. It can be a baker, banker, or candlestick maker. Maybe a full-time homemaker. Look at the Standard Occupational Classification System (SOC) for career ideas. SOC is the United States government system of classifying occupations.

- Understand it
- Care about it
- Symbolize it
- Think about it
- Decide it
- Orderly plan it
- Communicate it
- Team-connect it
- Learn it
- Remember it
- Be it
- Get better at it
- Become the best at it

 Cycle repeat as needed

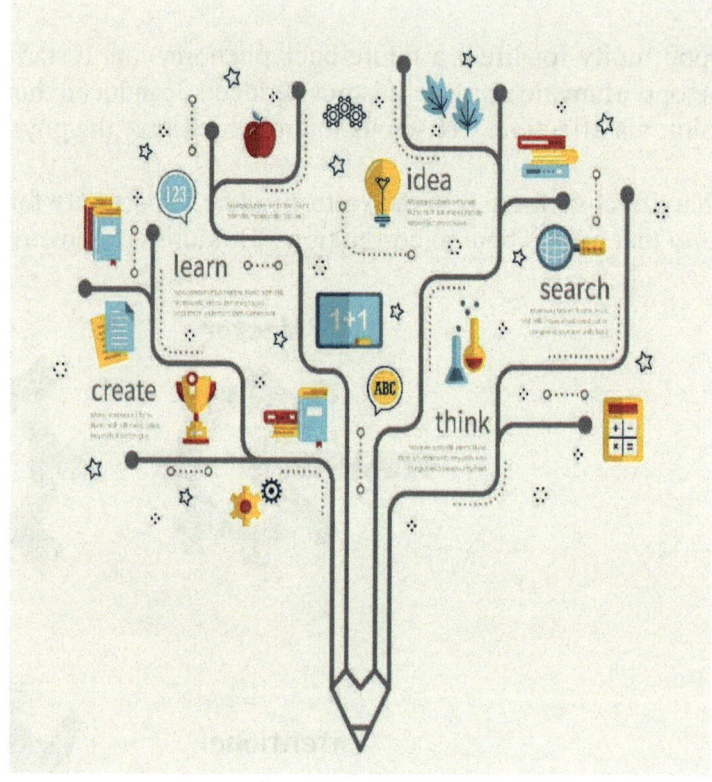

This is called *Partology*; it's how parts fit the whole. Partology is an intention-framed; planning, doing, reviewing, learning, and remembering thought-tool. It can be used for both things and ideas. Understand the whole, recognize what you have got, and then act to fill in the pieces.

_____
_____
_____
_____
_____

Pointing out the Partology. That is what a Conscious brain/mind can do.

HDSA Opportunity: Opportunity for life or death is the foundational verse of the Universe.

The Universe works one way. Underneath all events are four simultaneous logics, creating multi-logics. *HDSA multi-logics* is the universal glue. It frames any success and/or failure.

Each assembly or decay action occurs as a part moves in **Hierarchy**, via coordinated **Dimensions**, in a stepwise **Series**, as **Alternatives** are judged. There are four logics at work simultaneously.

Therefore, think HDSA "multi-logically" in the plan, communication, action, and situation response. HDSA multi-logical thinking makes you smarter. It links the right points of view.

Let's look at each of these logical methods individually and then as they are intentionally linked and used by your conscious awareness. Self is selected and maintained in HDSA multi-logics.

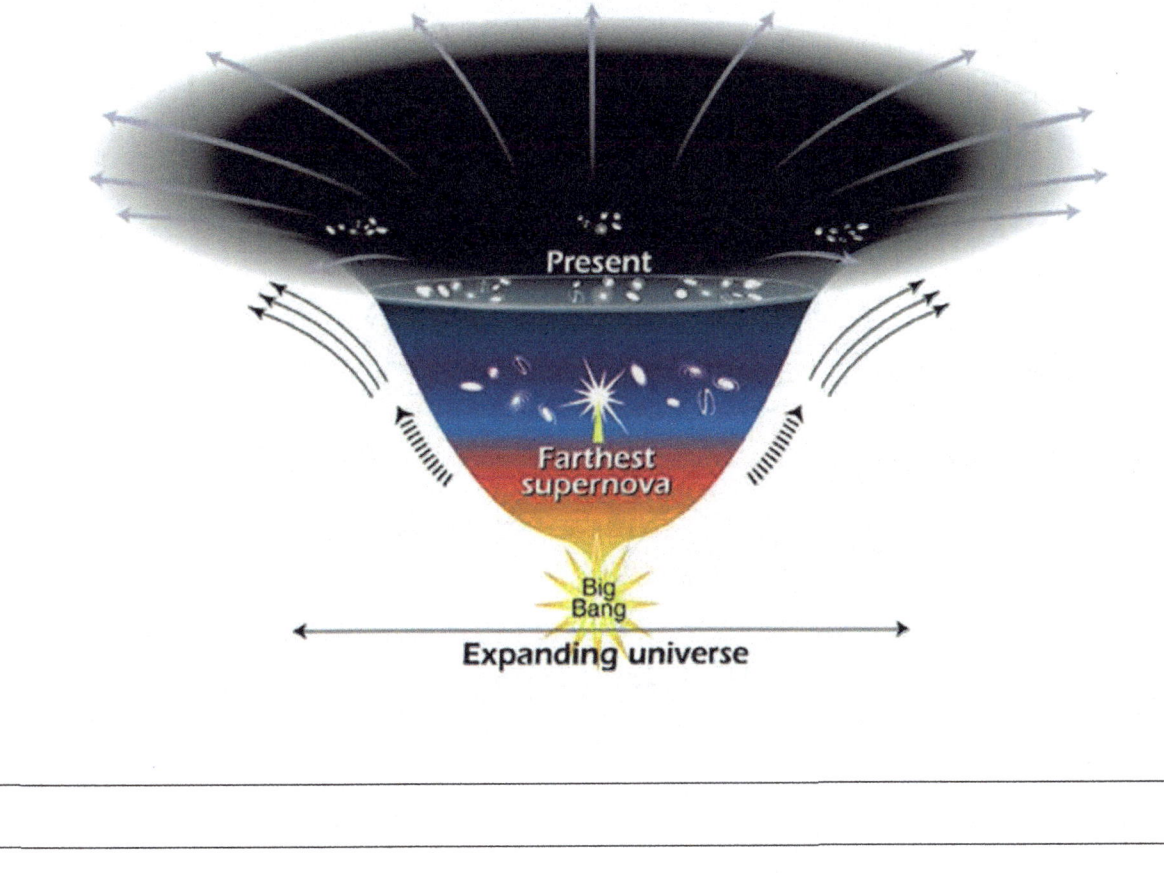

_____
_____
_____
_____
_____

The Universe is an HDSA multi-logical structure. So is your Conscious brain/mind.

21 Your Conscious brain/mind

Hierarchy: Some things are more important, at that time, than others.

There are many synonyms for the word hierarchy. An outline, taxonomy, Axiomatic sets and/or Venn diagrams all mean to set-up a logical hierarchy. All things fitting into other things is a recursive function for the assembly/decay life of each thing. These fits are hierarchical.

Hierarchy is the first logic because it sets up the order for the clear judgment of things. It is the first puzzle. Consciousness first judges, then it understands and does, to achieve a life goal.

Partological thought, understanding how and when parts go into and out of wholes, uses a recursive hierarchy. Partology maps in foreknowledge how pieces naturally fit into wholes.

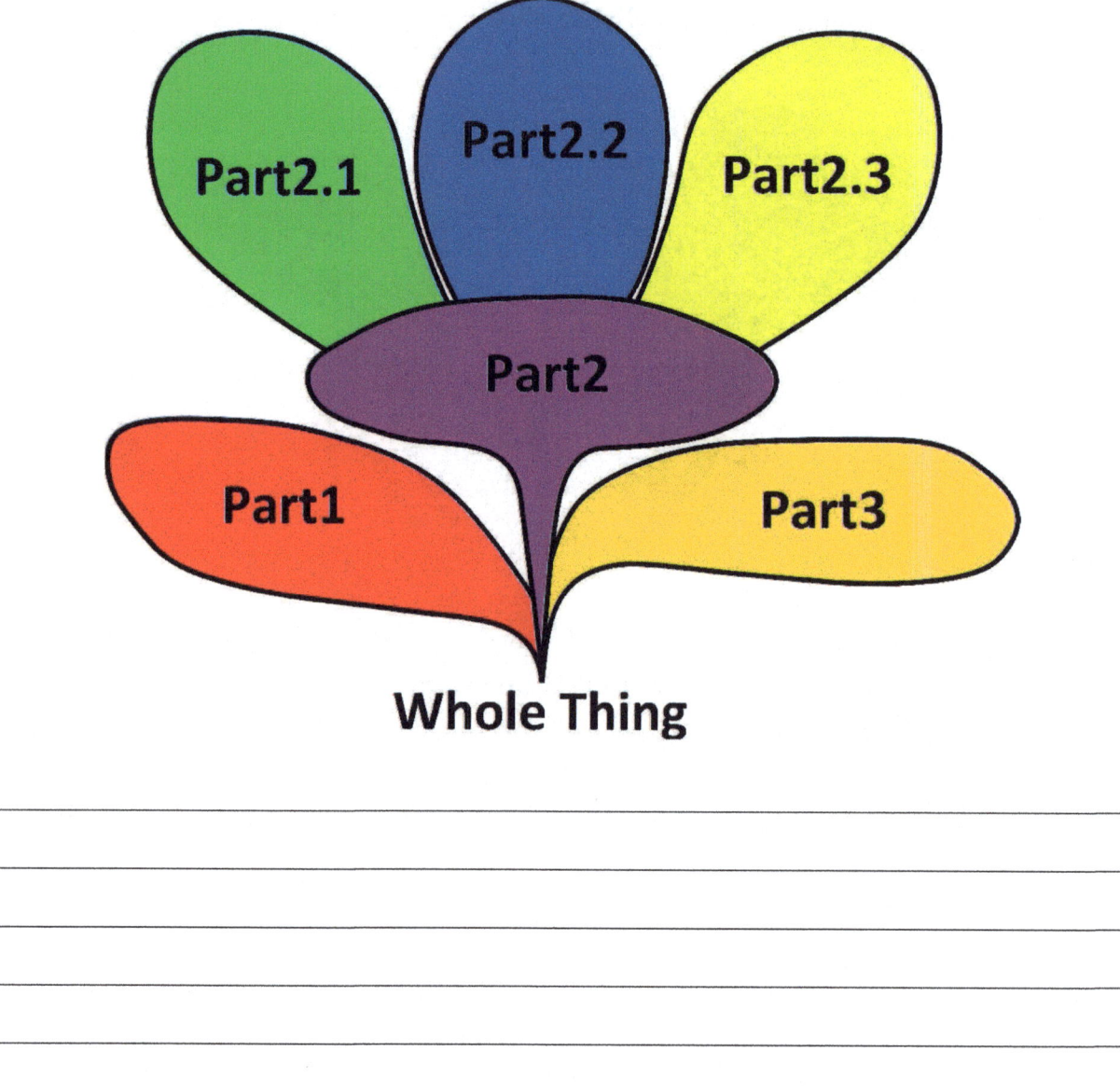

_____
_____
_____
_____
_____

In time, pieces connect and disconnect. Consciousness judges what to do when.

22 Your Conscious brain/mind

Dimensionality: How many things can you get done at the same time?

There are many simultaneous locations in expanding spacetime. Each physical part takes up a spacetime location. All of the relevant parts can be, and should be, consciously thought about using dimensional logic. Link same-time dimensions to improve thinking. Parts connect up. Each part, at that level, must fit at the same time. This occurs, and is defined, dimensionally.

The hierarchical, top-down logical organization can also be viewed dimensionally. This allows consciousness to plan and implement coordinated actions. That is smarter and more efficient.

Hierarchy and Dimensionality overlap logically. They align, creating stepped parallel operations in both space and time. More then gets done. Less time and energy are expended. That's smart.

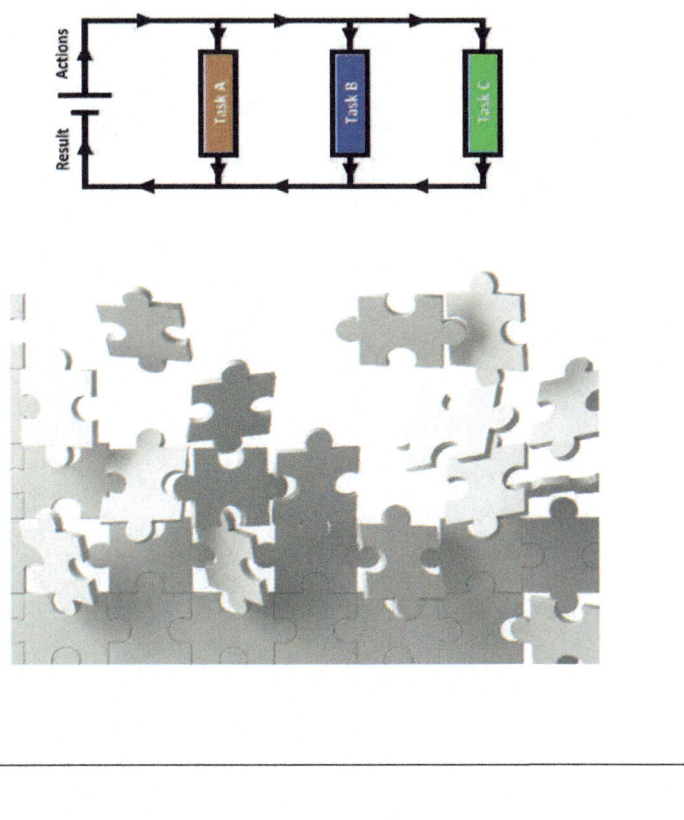

_____
_____
_____
_____
_____
_____

Dimensionality is used to plan more efficient simultaneous actions.

Seriality: At each point, take it step by step.

Judge what needs to be done via hierarchy. Plan simultaneous actions in dimensions. Assemble and decay in serial steps with quality checks.

The first two arrange the parts. The serial steps actually do the connect or disconnect actions.

Procedures and work instructions are stepwise instructions for a desired result. These planned behaviors act upon the multiple parts in a coordinated fashion; to connect or disconnect.

Part logical, Partological methods define the HDSA multi-logical framework for the efficient assembly or decay of any and all desired results. You can then get more for less.

_____
_____
_____
_____
_____

Now focus on the next step action with its quality checks.

24 Your Conscious brain/mind

Alternatives: Choose wisely for Life; yours, mine, and ours.

The first three logics (HDS) are driven by the physical Universe. They occur without conscious intervention. The final logic, Alternative decision-making, is a Life function. It starts with Self opportunity and continues to have greater influence as Life intelligence evolves and is Conscious brain/mind remembered into higher levels of insight and efficient behavior.

All things choose the best, most economical fits among alternatives. However, only living things intentionally choose to promote their and our lifetime. Life promotes itself in this conscious way.

This means we, the current intelligent things, create the future world in which we live. That's a sobering thought. We, the collective human intellect, make our Heaven or Hell here on earth.

_____
_____
_____
_____
_____

Choose what, how, where, why, and when. Choose for our lifetimes.

Dikw Symbolism: Data, information, knowledge, and wisdom (Dikw).

A Conscious brain/mind symbolizes HDSA-ordered reality. It does this to create and remember useful foreknowledge. The intellect symbols all fall into one of four Dikw categories.

1. *Datum* is one fact about an object. Data is a collection of facts.
2. *Information* is the logical correlation of data. It presents consistent trends.

Both **D**ata and **I**nformation are about the past. **K**nowledge & **W**isdom describe future behaviors.

3. *Knowledge* is stepped know-how.
4. *Wisdom* is knowing when to apply what know-how.

Partology/HDSA/Dikw are a set of ideas about creating clearer ideas. It's how cognition works.

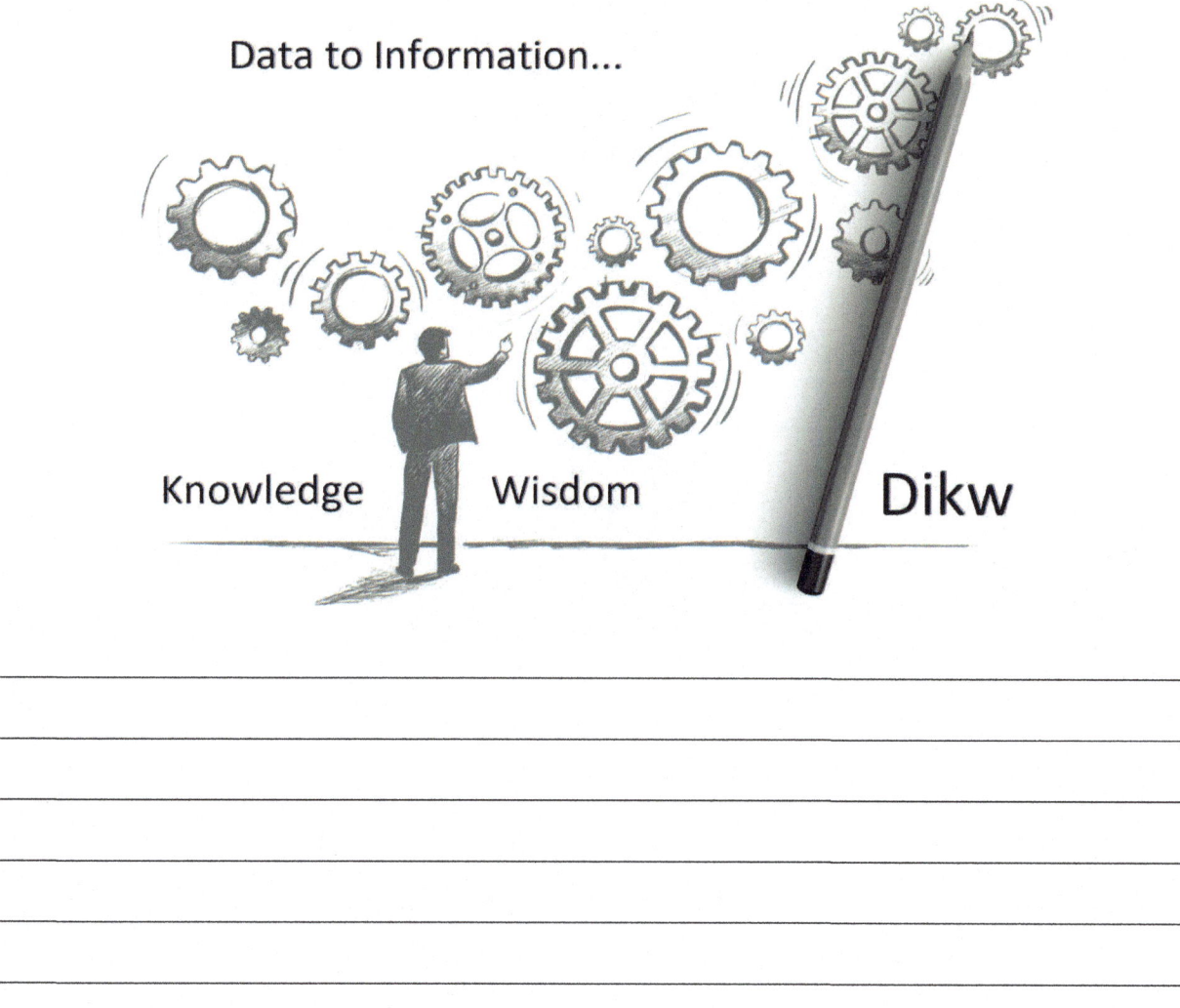

_____
_____
_____
_____
_____
_____

Data describes it. Information informs it. Knowledge knows it. Wisdom will choose it.

26 Your Conscious brain/mind

Homework Assignment: Now solve a problem that is important to you.

When framing a partological focus, useful ideas will intentionally align. This is like ideological gravity. Efficient idea alignment is a natural force created by the *for Life* opportunistic Universe.

Take the current issue of import to you. Name the whole of it. Post the Dikw pieces of it; those assembly or decay parts. Now place those identified points into the HDSA multi-logical frame.

Some of these points will be data; others will derive information. Other ideas will be knowledge (know-how) or wisdom (knowing when to perform a task). This makes you more conscious.

To know and get more: Dikw symbolize the HDSA multi-logical quanta. Order and symbolize those parts into a clear, understandable, and actionable Partology.

_____
_____
_____
_____
_____

Keep asking, "What is the next part question, at this level, in this domain?"

27 Your Conscious brain/mind

Think Again: A Conscious brain/mind improves the more you HDSA/Dikw think about it.

There is no such thing as good thinking. There is only *good re-thinking*. Before you act and use expensive resources (time, money, reputation, etc.), make sure that you have planned it right.

Dikw and HDSA are containers for thought. They frame the process of good, accurate thinking. The more you use these meta-thought tools, the smarter you will become. Eventually, it becomes second nature, an autonomic thinking process. Ideas become co-related from all points of view.

The more you think about it and re-meme it (ideologically refine it), the smarter you and your life plans will become. In this complicated and competitive world order, the quality of thought is the real Life-creating asset. Get good at thinking anew. It creates the future.

Identify, know, and link parts into your wholes. Then rethink what you think you know.

_____
_____
_____
_____
_____

Past students say you get it, bit by bit. Yourself builds its Self, in this way.

28 Your Conscious brain/mind

Truth is Power: The truth describes both what is and can be made better.

Knowing the truth, telling the truth, creating the truth, skewing the truth, new truths, applying the truth, researching the truth, building the truth, true documentation, co-relating the truth, and personally relating to truths; these are essential to Life more abundant.

Falsehoods die out in space over time. Truer ideas for Life advance humanity. The core and most essential Cognitive Scientific truth is that we can all get much smarter if we think like both the Universe and the Conscious brain/mind operate.

HDSA multi-logical alignment of Dikw symbolized Partology is the key truth of this book.

_____
_____
_____
_____
_____
_____

It's best to tell the truth because all statements are now recorded in cyberspace; forever.

Certified Metacognitions: For more insight, join www.Metacognitions.org

- Brain is physical
- Mind is ideological
- Consciousness is intentional
- a Self is subjectivity and objectively made-up by a Conscious brain/mind

The thing physical, informative, and intentional overlaps using the universal HDSA multi-logics to form Dikw memes (memes are many-to-many ideas that condense insights and decisions). A **meme** is an ideological gene. They are the evolutionary steps of cultured thought. They are culturally created, mentally remembered, used, improved, and then shared by a teacher.

Added intellect improves your and our lifetimes. If you know and think like this, you get smarter. There are many classes now being offered in Cognitive Science. To see an example of an online course, click **www.CogSci101.com.**

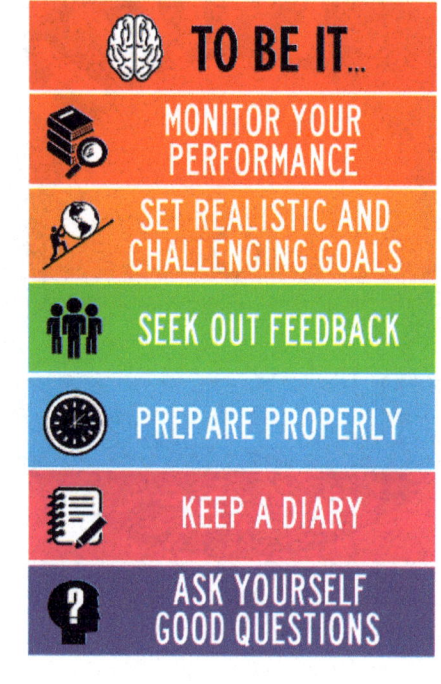

_____
_____
_____
_____
_____

The Metacognitions Society. We are step by step. We look up.

30 Your Conscious brain/mind

In Sum: Pure and simple truth is rarely pure and never simple. ~ Oscar Wilde

About 14 billion years ago, the Universe popped into existence; from nothing.

This Universe, that one multi-logical verse, started with a fixed amount of energy/matter (E=MC²) that is churning. It continues to churn in spacetime from the smallest parts (Quantum particles) up to the most massive chunks; the Black holes.

Along the way HDSA/Dikw meme-formatted, idea Self-selecting, conscious Life forms emerged from this churning formation of material things. These forms are the willful and intentional living plants, animals, and we humans.

Conscious thinking, for intended life, is now the most important formative force. It reforms energy and matter so as to live better, for longer, on less. Each Self is an idea preselected and then manifested.

It's clear, Heaven and Hell are made by us all. Also, what you don't know can hurt you a lot.

Get smarter for Life…

The metacognition contained in this book has one purpose. It is designed to help people get smarted.

You get it bit by bit. Please read the Cognitive Engineering examples that follow. Reference the glossary for the definition of terms.

You may send questions or comments to:
GaryDeines@Boutonics.com

Metacognition is thinking about how you think. To develop metacognition, to improve your metacognition, you must think about metacognition. Metacognition is the "framework" of how you think. It is more abstract. That makes it more influential over your entire thought process.

The most accurate form of metacognition is universal; it is defined by the Universe itself. That means it is the same for us all. The above ideas define the structure of this metacognition. Each is a piece of the HDSA/Dikw Partology. Think about each term individually. Then link them together. This is like knowing about anything. The parts make up the whole.

Keep in mind; we do not program you. You program you. It is your life to think about, define, and live. Instead, Cognitive Science will provide insights into how to do this. If you take a metacognitive approach to learning, remembering, and intending; then your situation mind-sets become more powerful. You become more aligned for the quality of your and our lifetime.

The examples that follow, and the glossary of terms, will help to further the development of an accurate metacognition in your Conscious brain/mind. Good thinking for us all.

31 Your Conscious brain/mind

Cognitive Engineering Examples

Applied Cognitive Science is called Cognitive Engineering. Cognitive Engineers take the explicit CogSci theories and methods into an application for a specific mental situation. To better explain the science, what follows are a few practical Cognitive Engineering examples.

Teaching Smarter

A few years ago, I was asked by Northeastern University here in Boston to transfer the insights contained in Partology (that HDSA/Dikw symbolism) to their university. It was decided that I would get paid to teach an advance thinking/webbing course in the Communications department. They assigned a co-professor to take notes and instantiate the knowledge inside the university.

The course was successful; seniors and a few juniors. After the course was completed, as we were all standing around with cokes and coffee, three students approached the co-professors. The tall male stopped and said, "Professor Deines, I want to thank you for the knowledge that you gave us, my dad has got me a summer job web-automating the Quality documentation in his firm."

Then a second student, a woman, said, "I also want to thank you. I'm applying for a very competitive job in an NYC Ad agency, and they commented on how I web-organized my resume, placed it on a thumb drive, linked in that 'tiny' web-server, and submitted it as Conscious Software". It ran as they plugged it in. That made me different, more technically skilled."

Then the third student, another woman, said, "Yes, I also want to thank you. I just got a summer intern job at a small ad agency here in Boston because I spoke about organizing 'parts' of an Ad campaign and then web-automating the communications."

I thanked them all, they left, and the co-professor looked at me and said, "Do you know what just happened?" I stopped for a moment and then said slowly, a bit confused, I think so. He then went on to say that he had been teaching for 12 years at the University level and never had any students come up at the end of a course and thank him for the knowledge that he had shared. I did not know what to say, and we went back to our previous conversation.

In walking to my car, I am trying to figure out how Universities can take time and money to teach students stuff that they cannot use. I think it's how I link true new theory into a practical application that makes the difference. Partology allows me to link solid theory to real practice. With it, I can see a bit farther; my thoughts are more inclusive. That's how it makes us all smarter.

Practical Partology

A father came home to find his wife and fourth-grade daughter arguing about a piece of blank paper. The daughter had been given a homework assignment to write about Abraham Lincoln. No words were yet penned, and the family tension was rising.

The father said, "OK, let's look at this in parts. Daughter, you know how to write a sentence (subject, verb, objects). You need to write three paragraphs, each with three sentences. That's nine sentences. That's all you need to do to complete the assignment. You read the book on Lincoln. What is the first thing you want to say?"

"Dad, did you know that Abraham Lincoln was born in a log cabin?" "Yes," said dad, "That could be your first sentence. Now, what else did you find interesting about Lincoln?" The daughter said, "He became President of the United States of America, and that will be my next sentence."

As the fourth-grade writer's block was undone, using parts of a whole, the father thought, "I wonder if my daughter will one day be sharing this partological writing method with her children?"

A New Meme

Your Career Manifest Destiny (CMD) has recently become a new cultural meme. Remember, a gene is a life instruction, situationally placed into a physical DNA structure, to manifest itself in the subsequent cellular growth of a living organism. Genes are intelligent for the physical life of that thing. They are physically passed on, to the new living thing, at embryo cell conception.

A meme is not physical but ideological in its construction. Memes are inculcated in a culture, learned, and remembered by a society. Memes are passed on symbolically by the desired and remembered ideology of a specific culture. The culture outside the thing knows and remembers a pattern of life behavior that is good for all lives; that becomes a named meme. The culture uses the memorialized meme to inculcate the new humans entering into their society of things. That is the symbolic role of a meme, as it transfers life intelligence from generation to generation.

Your CMD is a new meme. Here is one example of its use. A smart woman now sells. One of her new customers asked, in casual dialogue, "Judy, what is your Career Manifest Destiny?" Judy responded with, "What do you mean?" The customer explained, and Judy thought, "I would be happy being a partner in an Ad Agency. That is the work that I like to do. Plus, I'd be making a lot more money than now."

The customer then said, "How would you do that, the steps?" Judy is now working on that process using Partology; step-by-step. Finding and following your Career Manifest Destiny is a new meme that can help all people at any life stage.

Note: Meme Marketing is a new marketing method. It is based on uncovering, in advance, the essential meme ideas that will rule the future of your specific business domain (the next "it"). Once uncovered and articulated, the company uses an integrated system of technology-plus-people to message-market into that new, emerging consumer insight, desire, and buying behavior.

Commonwealth Errors

The Commonwealth of Massachusetts, the Legislature, recently passed a law stating that Zoning density would be doubled within .5 miles of any public transportation stop. Their goal was to increase the use of public transportation (trains, buses, planes).

The doubling of zoning density in the seaside community of Gloucester, MA, would have a profound impact on the quality of life. A small group of people came together under the idea that "Governing of the people" is different from "Government by the people," and they prefer the latter. They then planned, as a focused group, to part the pieces in order to build their political influence. The first step was "in the community" of local citizens. A team was built. Then they influenced local politicians to change their support and vote Chapter 40r down. That step was completed. Now they are taking aim at the Commonwealth as a whole.

What built this successful movement? They thought about it as a "sequence of parts" that would make up a whole. They aligned one piece at a time in the proper order and then built it into a pre-planned whole. Each SIPO step was easy. Situation IPO (input>process>output) was their recurring method. Now the whole, that pieced alignment of their political movement, has power.

Rome was not built in a day. It was, like this movement is now building, a set of idea-behavior aligned parts that powered into a whole. This group of people has found how to practically invigorate grassroot democracy. Or as many states-men and women have said, "There is great power in the democratic process."

The next piece being added they called "compromise." In their charter, they will clearly define the who, what, when, how, where, and why they compromise with others. They want this foreknowledge generally discussed, decided, and documented in advance of its need. That is another smart ideological piece to think about, discuss, and add before it is needed.

Personalize Public Schools

Northampton, Massachusetts, is an interesting place. It is located in western MA, west of Worcester and before the Berkshires. Within a five-mile drive, there are five major Universities, including UMass, the flagship public university in the Commonwealth. Northampton is a smart, eccentric, eclectic, laid-back, proactive liberal city. The Public school system is staffed with many professional educators. It is also known for excellent Private schools like Deerfield Academy and the Campus School of Smith College.

A few years ago, a new student entered kindergarten in the public school, and midmorning, the students were told that "It's now time to go get your blanket, go to your mat, close your eyes, and take a nap." One 5-year-old student said, "I don't think so." A discussion ensued, with the teachers guiding this student to his mat with his blanket.

That student, which we will call Harvey, covered himself with the blanket on his mat and began to inch-worm crawl under his blanket, eventually hitting another student taking a nap. The teachers admonished the behavior as <u>bad</u> and placed Harvey on his mat, only to have him crawl away again.

This went on for three days. The teachers could not inculcate Harvey's proper behavior, labeled it "bad," and then called the parents. The parents understood the problem and offered their support. A number of things were tried, to no success, and finally, a 504 IEP (these are MA individual student education accommodation plans, put in writing) was set up to resolve the issue. The solution was to place a container of books and toys away from the children sleeping, where Harvey could go and do his stuff during naptime.

two peacock mantis shrimp

Here are two of his sketches. Harvey proudly tells you that it's two "peacock mantis shrimp." It turns out that Harvey is not "bad" but a very smart five-year-old.

Public school systems must have standards, no question. However, kids are individuals. Just because they desire and need to learn in a different way, other subjects, we should not teach them that they are "bad." As this story was related to me, I became very impressed with the public school system in Northampton, MA. It is a perfect example of the culture adapting to the individual; for the good of us all.

It will be interesting to see how reasoned Harvey becomes in his lifetime. Also, how "group civilized." For efficient life, the content must properly fit into its context and vice versa. Cognitive friction on either side is to be avoided.

How You Think

In physics, in the mathematical modeling of how physical parts behave individually and in groups, they have a number of interesting thought-tools. One is the "many-body problem" that states all parts (or wave points) affect all other parts; in varying degrees. Another is "Ground States," which try to simplify the formulations. Another quantum computational method is the Density-functional Theory (DFT). Also, Quantum Field theory, that relative geometry, attempts to calculate the simultaneous, multiple a/effects of parts or points on all others; in a pre-defined and clearly stated domain. A/effect is a simultaneous effect and its corresponding, same time effect.

Each of these methods, all current mathematical methods, are not completely accurate; but statistical. The world is too complex for one mathematical method to be accurate all the time. So, a specific math method must be defined to fit the Conscious brain/mind. This is called the Tesimal numbering of causations, as Data science accounted.

People do not think of equality. Instead, we all think about getting ahead; to better ourselves and others. The purpose of intelligence, in an intended situation, is to better the outcome. If leaving things well enough alone is the decision, and not doing anything new, then that decision is the better outcome to get ahead.

In Cognitive Science, we call this "Causal Mathematics" and have created a new type of number (a Tesimal) to more accurately model that formulation. The equal sign (=) is dropped for the causal signs of assembly < and decay >. This "causation" is a recipe for intended success. It looks like this:

I now want $< Part1 + Part2 - Part3 \times Part4 << Part4.1 + Part4.2$ etc.

In causation, you form a map of the nested and ordered part additions and subtractions. This is clear thinking. The more precisely you have identified the elements, with alternatives, and placed them into an HDSA multi-logical format using the Tesimal numbering method; the clearer and more accurate your situational thoughts become. That is how you think to get smarter.

Note: What is a Tesimal number, and how does it differ from a Natural number? Tesimal numbers simultaneously map hierarchy, dimensionality, seriality, and alternative logics into a single numbering string. Take a large Natural number, say 10^{10}, and allocate the 100,000-place range for mapping hierarchy, the next 10 number places for up to ten simultaneous dimensions, the next 100 places for serial action, and the final 10-digit places to number available alternatives, by serial point location, in rank order.

Left-pack all numbers and do not use those number places that are not needed in your causation. Now associate each number that needs to be used with a specific Dikw part symbol. In this way, the Dikw symbols are HDSA-ordered most tersely. Via this roulette (a math term), this is how the Conscious brain/mind creates its efficient way to format memory.

Intelligent Mating

One student of Cognitive Science, and a member of the Metacognition Society, was still in college (2022), taking an advanced Psychology course from a well-respected professor; with an international reputation. One day, the student approached the professor to discuss what he had learned from his "Your Conscious brain/mind" training.

The professor listened intently and then became a little riled up. "What bull," the professor retorted, "I am very well-versed in Psychology, Neurophysiology, Philosophy, and Cognitive studies, and nobody knows how the mind works. To claim otherwise is false." The student then tried to explain "conduction", describing how a mindset can become "dogmatically opinionated," and the professor got even more agitated.

This was not good. So, the student said let's try one; let's see if this idea called "Partology" can help you get something you want? If it does, if that scientific experiment works, then we might have something of value here. The professor jokingly responded, "find me a new life mate," and the conversation ended. The student thought more about this. The professor was single and wanted to find the right life mate.

A few days later, using Partology (how parts go into and out of wholes), the student gave the professor a written note that said, "To find a new life mate, you must (1) first define the characteristics of the type of woman that you desire, (2) then determine how you must adjust "who and what you are" to fit their needs, and (3) finally you should casually show up to where that type of desired life mate is to be found; their watering hole." In short, part the idea pieces together for an efficient and influential mating result.

Four months later, that professor announces that a well-known European professor of Psychology, a woman, has agreed to come to his university for six-months and co-author a new book. It seems like a worthwhile match was made by just thinking anew about it. This is the power of the partological thought-tool. The pieces can more explicitly fit the whole. Planned results become clearer bit-by-bit. Results are built via coordinating the parts into the desired whole.

You must be open. Let go of what you know to "conduct" more life intelligence.

Scientific Mysticism

A colleague of mine, Dr. Chris Wachsmuth, out of Germany, is taking a slightly different approach to pinpointing the foundational essence of the Conscious brain/mind. He searches for the start of conscious awareness, as both an ideological and material event, in the Big bang; actually before the Big bang. In more common terms, this is "Intelligent Design" before Natural Selection. Dr. Wachsmuth wants to understand and channel the power of that Universal opportunity for "the good life."

Basically, E-MC² holds that matter cannot be created or destroyed, only converted. Relativistic Cosmology states that one Big bang created all the matter in this World, and it has been expanding out in space over time. Dr. Wachsmuth is toying with the idea that conscious, intentional creation continues to add more matter, and this process is accelerating. It's his causal source of Dark Energy and Dark Matter.

He puts Consciousness (intentional awareness and behaviors) at the center as the cause of this more materialization. This is a mind-over-matter ideology. It would say that Consciousness is larger than the Universe. His belief says that conscious things make up the World anew; each day.

I include this as an example of how open dialogue, and not a prejudicial academic approach, will lead us all into a more creative and useful future. Remember, knowledge is, by definition, prejudice; knowledge is a prejudgment. We all must get beyond what we know to know more. I'm open to Dr. Wachsmuth's train of thought.

Truth Resolves Trumpism

It appears that the USA, and the World order, is undergoing a radical change. People are increasingly dissatisfied with their leaders. In the USA, this started with Ross Perot (in 1992, the independent Perot garnered 19% of the presidential vote) and has evolved into we-the-people electing Trump as President in 2016. Bannon and Trump recognized that this undercurrent of "political leadership hatred" could be channeled into votes. As generally self-operating, egotistic people (America First), they spoke to that audience and won; for a brief period.

Now we have the Trump wannabes. They are on the committee and at the outspoken forefront to stop the "weaponization of government." Think about this for a moment. We are electing people that want to neuter the government. They do not want to repair or improve the system. Is this not oxymoronic and a violation of their sworn duty? What, government by-and-for the people, is a bad thing? When did that become a popular idea?

Cognitively, with the mass persuasive power of the Internet, this is a very interesting time for humanity. The Conscious brain/mind is developed by repetitively firing the same associated boutons, creating a specific symbolized mindset. Once created, it is hard to change. Liars know and use this CogSci fact.

However, the truth will set you free. Truths, well telling the truth, will work both short and long-term. Just keep thinking and speaking the truth. Good government is just that. It's truly good for us all. Good governments efficiently solve real problems. We all should vote for people that do that.

Be smart, not dumb; we thereby can collectively live better for longer on less. Each lifetime can be an optimum conduction, an individual creation, and a work of art. That individual action, each person being their best, will sum up into a very powerful country for all the World to admire.

All Thinking Is Cognitive

Below is an email dialogue with a friend. All that we all do, both in spoken words and actions, is cognitive. It is for a good or bad intended Life purpose.

Even the simplest thing or action can upgrade conscious awareness; if you just take the time to cognitively think it through. Below I get even better at family, and so may Peter.

> PS: How was the family reunion? What was re-unioned?

Peter   Mar 7, 2023, 7:28 PM
to me

All fourteen family members spent a few days skiing together at our place in Vermont.

> Peter
>
> **Hi Peter,**
>
> As you know, I like to understand words at their depth. This is because they are so life causal. Words affect thoughts and action automatically. We should all think more about our words (imho).
>
> This union and re-union word is very interesting. After asking you the question, I started thinking about what that word means to me. "Family" is a key word and action in my family (like in yours).
>
> Our union is family. So, this thought, my question to you was really for me. It got me thinking better about my unionizing actions in my family. There is behavior improvement in that thought.
>
> Yes, a bit obscure. It's what we Cognitive Scientists think about. The mathematical, logical, and intuitive union of more conscious cogs; which are words. -g

Efficient Workings

One person uses Partology and HDSA multi-logics as a recurring daily guide. She has named all the things that define her area of responsibility (Name1, Name2, Name#...) and prioritized them by number. If she has a Name1 task to do, she will pick that up and focus on completion. If not, she looks for the Name2 items to do, etc. When she does not have any named and numbered tasks to do, she focuses on learning anew and/or building stronger relationships.

That's her system for the optimum allocation of the scarcest resource called "time". It is very efficient.

This is <u>not</u> the FIFO (first in, first out) logical structure of a computer operating system. Instead, conscious awareness always judges priorities before any action. We could call this MIAF and mean the Most-Important-Action-First. Look up, to decide, then look down to focus on the completion of a task. That is intelligent for life.

The MIAF cognitive operating structure is seen throughout all conscious living things. Observe a robin pecking for food in your backyard. They peck, then they look up and around, then they look down and peck again. They are judging to peck or to fly away before they act. This thinking method is for their life.

In CogSci, we call this Judge and Do (JAD). Think about the judgments you must make and the follow-up action to take. Identify, order, and link these two into a Partological system of thought. Make this autonomic; make it a situation-dependent automated habit. JAD foreknowledge improves performance by saving life time.

How to Judge in the Face of Uncertainty.

In terms of lifetime success, judgment is about five-times more important than action. Therefore, spend more time in the judgment phase, especially with new and unfamiliar situations.

A stockbroker is now using a partological system that he, over the years, has created for himself. It guides how he invests money (his own and the money entrusted to him by others). His investing system takes a lot of time. He thinks about a lot of economic factors, both short and long-term. Each of these factors is weighed in making an investment decision. Each factor is ordered and prioritized logically in "clicks". Then the final decision is made by sitting back and using intuitive logic. The final decision is created from a "felt" conducted jump.

The recurring key to his particular investment system is "innovation". That is his focus. He is an expert at finding the best-and-brightest in the most promising emerging economic fields. Having this proven system, that has worked for him for years, is his real business asset.

How do you judge what to do? Are you selfish, other-ish, or somewhere in between (the flexible space where you should be)? Do you seek out experts to learn from or always try to go it alone? Do you listen to experts without taking your own experience into consideration? Do you stay on-point, both in the short or long-term, using material space-time frames?

In terms of Life quality and duration, judgment is about five-times more important than action. Create your own cognitive system that judges. Send an email to GaryDeines@Boutonics.com that describes this multi-logical method. We'll namelessly share it with others; via the Metacognitions Society. We always act to protect individual identities while we share useful cognitive insights.

Experience Create, Memorize, Situation Load, and Consciously Act; Point by Point

Let's summarize. Consciousness is a metaphysical process, an agency of Self. It arises from mental symbology that co-relates how matter a/effects each other physically in space over time.

As such, consciousness is a causal agent, made more so by the HDSA logical overlapping and Dikw aligning of pre-material symbolic forms (forms are what matters), that recursively network. These symbolic networks connect, as bouton pathways, creating situation intended packaged foreknowledge.

Whoo, that is a mind full. We never said that consciousness, the complete system, was simple. Instead, we said that the Conscious brain/mind could understand the nature of consciousness (itself) and, in so doing, learn how to think and act better for life; yours, mine, and ours.

So: taught-or-learned experience feedback creates, bouton connected memories (those part chunked connected symbols) that are intentionally loaded by the situation (into mental working memory) and consciously acted out, point by point. That opportunity for advancing Life intellect is provided by the Universe and recursively conducted by the Self-conscious agency. Your life opportunity precedes its reality. The feedback, provided by the new behavior acted out in the physical world, is then mentally observed for a more accurate statistical calculation (Data Science) and then re-summarized into the bouton instantiated memory memes, for future reference.

This is how the Conscious brain/mind works, as a metaphysical agency, changing the future course of reality. Each situation-implemented intention alters the physical world a small bit, creating another level of evolution toward a living Heaven or Hell for humans. Know this and you will get smarter in Life for us all.

This HDSA/Dikw partological conscious insight of the situation intended Self-agency has been described partially in many ways before. The Scientific method, PDCA in Quality Control, Language structures, logic, religions, various mathematics, etc., all say this insight from their limited viewpoint. Cognitive Science, a more eclectic science, is just explaining this pattern of intellect more accurately. That added accuracy is what makes you smarter.

Let me simplify. You have a Self-agency, a bouton conscious awareness that recursively connects ideas for the Life of us all. Know how to HDSA/Dikw do this, that multi-logical overlapping of symbols, and you get smarter in your lifetime. The more you align the parts of your consciousness with real Life opportunities, the better our world becomes for us all.

Partology Poetry

The Partological thinking method, that form of metacognition, answers and links the who, what, why, how, where, and when questions. **Who**; you. **What**; learn HDSA Dikw. **Why**; to get smarter. **How**; bit by bit. **Where**; everywhere. **When**; always. Partology thinking sets up a more conscious framework. It is a very useful and generally applicable metacognition.

Here is an example of poetry written using Partological thinking. "**Partology is**... Pithy phrases, purposely packing a punch, punctuated with pregnant pauses." What makes this poem partological? It is terse, consistent, and makes one point.

Partology is "it's from bits". It is used to efficiently link, to clearly and intentionally link, the ideological bits. That more accurate and purposeful ideology is what makes you more conscious. It is true. It is simple. It is civically moral. It encircles and properly enforces the whole; any whole, regardless of the parts. It is the natural way to think clearly.

If you know how your Conscious brain/mind works physically, those part-aligned bouton bits, then you can take conscious, ideological action to make it work better. You can now program you! The HDSA Dikw linked symbols are intelligently formatted, and easily remembered, for your life. You program you. Get better at doing this.

Smarter Generations to Come

I am pleased to announce that the average IQ in the USA keeps rising each year (except these last few covid years). This has a twofold cause: (1) better cultural memes and (2) Internet communications. The memes, the culturally developed and instantiated insights and ideologies are getting better (we learn from our mistakes), and this in-formation is now better organized, indexed and accessible at the push of a few browser keystroke buttons.

For example, the day after I heard that Lucien (my 5-year-old grandson) was writing a book using one of my original ideas (or so I contend) I posted this concern to the family chat. This is communicating in real-time.

> **Gary Deines** 2 min
>
> I am a bit concerned. Yesterday I heard that Lucien was writing a book and he seems to be using my word/image co-relation method. I do not know if this is morphogenesis, "spookies action at a distance" or Einstein's comment on "shade your eyes while you plagiarize". So the race is now on. Who will get their book published first!
>
> PS: Granted, Lucien being an illustrator, starts with the image and I with the words. This is different. I, being a Cognitive Scientist, start with the words and then go find and license the image. From what I hear, Lucien is doing the illustrations first and actually having someone else do the words. Maybe his "picture" before the 1,000 words is a better approach to creating understandable knowledge transfer.
>
> PPS: Another issue; at 5 years old, is it appropriate for Lucien to be illustrating and authoring a book. What life experience will be left to him when he gets to be a 70+ year old septuagenarian. What, he's going to walk on water, solve climate change, end world hunger, make everyone moral? Yes, I do have a lot of confidence in these future generations.

As of yet, his book has no title. Here is one of Lucien's illustrations for the book. According to him, it is Leafcutter ants; above and below ground (illustrated March of 2023).

How Do You Eat an Elephant?

One "Your Conscious brain/mind" reader, published in an earlier form via a set of papers, was having a very hard time amassing the money needed to buy a home for their growing family. Each month, most of their joint income was going to pay a very high apartment rent. They could not save money as fast as house prices were increasing. Each month they were falling farther behind. The financial equation parts, as they understood, were mathematically stacked against them. Or was that really the case?

What to do? They, both husband and wife, started to think anew, step-by-step. House prices are increasing faster than they were saving money. If they do nothing, then owning a home will become even more expensive. So, a new action was <u>now</u> required. That was the first bit of new factual insight.

Next, how much money was needed for the down payment? Their "dream home", in their "ideal community" was not cheap. Over $80,000 was needed as the minimal down payment, and they had $35,000. Maybe, they thought, we should not buy our dream home first but a starter-house that might need a little fix-me-up work. Let's eat this big elephant strategically, one bit-step at a time.

So, the real estate search took on a new perspective. Let's buy a home somewhere close by, in a less costly town, fix it up, and then sell it. Let's use that money made, and banking investment experience, to then buy (1) our dream home or (2) another fix-up home opportunity to raise the needed funds. That plan made sense.

This could work because their one child was not old enough to go to the local schools. Therefore, they could buy a home in a less desirable community as a starter.

In their case, there was only one fixer-upper home step that was needed. The first house bought appreciated by $45,000 in two and a half years with their fix-up addition. They then bought the home of their dreams, in the town they desired, close to their relatives and friends.

You get smarter, you learn to think in a partological way, step by step. Those small bouton bits assimilate into the more intelligent and abstract wholes. That is how it goes. This is what the "Partology" metacognition does.

What is a Deinian?

A Deinian is a unit of Life. Before I explain, it's useful to search YouTube for Max Planck's 1942 video where he describes his life work in Thermodynamics; how matter decays via entropy.

https://www.youtube.com/watch?v=9hzw622nMls

A Deinian is the inverse. It is artful, is artropic (to coin a new word). It is how Life assembles itself, process-part by process-part, to be more efficient and joyful. Keep in mind that Cognitive Science is a Life Science.

Here is an example of a Deinian. Last night, while taking a shower, I got shampoo soap in one eye. It stung, and I thoroughly washed it out. This morning I woke up with a little dried-up fluid in the corner of my eye. That mechanism is an evolved Deinian. The fluids that protect the eye from foreign substances, in the night, encased the remaining offensive chemicals and flushed them out of the eye. This is a Situation, Input>>Process>>Output (SIPO) behavior for the life of my eye. Deinian math, using Tesimal numbering, can accurately describe it.

Here is another Deinian for my life. When hungry, I eat. That is the situation action. The food goes into my mouth, chomped down into more digestible parts, and swallowed. The intestines use chemicals to abstract the useful cellular nutrients from the biomass, and the bowels move to excrete the waste. This is another Deinian because it's a SIPO for Life. Deinians model each stage from many different viewpoints. They are HDSA/Dikw symbolically modelled.

Here is another mentally memorized Deinian. When I hit a tennis ball down the line to Bob Kershaw, and I see Bob position himself to hit his backhand crosscourt (as usual), I will start moving in that direction before his swing. This is a statistical SIPO. It is foreknowledge that I've learned by playing against Bob over the last 20 years.

How many SIPO Deinians does it take to make up a human being? How are they integrated? How are they instantiated? When are they triggered? How are they improved for a lifetime? Some Deinians use chromosomal genes, and others are culturally instantiated, remembered, and taught as ideal memes; and then stored in bouton memory. All are integrated and aligned agents for and creating my Self. SIPO formations explain the "hard problem" of self.

A Deinian is to "assembly" what entropy is to decay. They are both stepwise processes, only in the inverse. Boutons assemble using memorized Situation IPO behaviors. That is the source of Consciousness.

Note: Classical mechanics is to Quantum mechanics what Quantum mechanics is to Conscious mechanics. Conscious mechanics is our next essential step in understanding Worldwide causality. It is "intentional" for Life; yours, mine, and ours. Structurally it uses learned SIPOs, HDSA organized to cause future behaviors. For more insight, see www.ConsciousMechanics.com.

More Impact

A public servant, the director of the Property Assessors Office in a town north of Boston, MA, took Partology into an innovative direction; she web-automated it. She used the selecting and HDSA ordering of Assessor Dikw points (on web pages) to increase the impact her department had upon their community. It was not AI. Instead, it was the Real Intelligence (RI) of the department that was placed on the Web. Fewer people could then get more accomplished.

Her department, the town Property Assessors office, is traditionally understaffed. As real estate and property taxes started rising, the number of phone calls from townspeople increased to the point that they had a difficult time answering the questions, distributing the forms, collecting the applications, processing the work, and publishing the results.

It dawned upon her that this community dialogue was partological and that each of these activities could be a bit of a website. So, instead of saying and doing each thing for each person, they said it once on web pages. Now when a person calls with a request, they listen and say, "Yes, I can help. Give me your email address, and I'll send you a link where you can get the information to fill out the forms you will need. If you have any difficulty, call us back."

By putting the intellectual answers into web-pages, that are easy to follow (stepwise), her people now say it once to the computer and let that web-automated, partological organized intelligence do most of their work.

Size of Consciousness

After a lecture, a student came up to me and asked, "How big is Consciousness?" I said, "Really big." She then said, "No, I'm asking a real question. You say that consciousness is a real thing. Things have a measurable size. So, it would help me if I knew how big this real thing called Consciousness really is?"

OK, a useful question for a Cognitive scientist. Consciousness can encompass the smallest particle, the whole Universe, and each subset in between. So, it is the biggest thing we know. It is probably larger than the Universe itself. Life is the "one verse of the Universe," and Consciousness is its most useful behavior-calculating handmaiden.

Consciousness grows in size by naming and co-relating symbols. Some people, using HDSA/Dikw Partology, will expand the size of their conscious ability. Actually, they more intelligently use and apply their conscious resources. HDSA/Dikw Partology is designed to adapt to their Life opportunities.

We can look at this "size of consciousness" question from neurophysiology. Each Conscious brain/mind is endowed at birth with approximately 80 billion neurons. Each mature neuron develops ~1,200 bouton connections. So, a person has about one trillion bouton connection bits that compute in context. Boutons look at their current "intent" and the bouton community "extents" at the same time. This doubles the many-body problem to the many-many body problem.

Finally, a bouton in its "Intentional field" is polar (on/off) and pointed in both degrees and magnitude. So, each bouton quantized its range of influence internally and via external forces. That spherical variation of a one-trillion bouton bit computer creates a very large field for recording, deciding, and acting. Infinity is the size of this potential variation.

This means that the size of Consciousness, its potential Field of intelligent play as an intentional computer for Life, is almost the size of Life itself; past, present, and future. It's the biggest thing I know.

That is why it has taken Science so long to figure out how a Conscious brain/mind works. We are just beginning to understand its mechanism. It's a "Combinatorics mathematics" that is very convoluted in both the coming and its going (a/effect).

What is a Bouton?

The idea of a bouton is "recursive" throughout the three Conscious brain/mind layers. It is used to describe the physical, ideological, and intentional concept of cross-fitness. Boutons connect.

A bouton (button) is a neuronal growth, closing the synapse, that controls action potential firing or not; it's a decision gate. A bouton is one wave-form overlapping with others, either standing or moving. A bouton is a bit of an idea. A bouton is the whole idea. A bouton is ideal; the best idea to be selected. A bouton is a context. A bouton is a piece of content. A bouton is real, ideal, and intentional, all at the same time. The Universe is a bouton. A single quantized energy wave, like a photon, is a bouton. Black holes are massive, energetic, gravity-pulling dense boutons in spacetime. The Conscious brain/mind is boutonized. Your CBM is an on-point integrated bouton processing machine. An individual CBM is also a bouton from another perspective.

A bouton is an ideological quantum, is based on Intent mechanics, and can be mathematically modeled using Deinian a/effect mathematical causations. They are the content and also the context.

How can a bouton (a button) be all of these things? You must think about it. Then send me an email when you have got it. Boutons make up your lifetime; as decision steps on stages. Each person should get good at this integrated, intentional, symbolizing way of thought. Better life; that is the recurring point under bouton examination.

What do buttons do? They fit and connect things forcefully. Anything that does that is a bouton; it is part of a Partology. Boutons line up for life or death. You get to choose. Choose your button parts wisely. That is the overall point of a boutonized Partology.

Dikw Example

Any domain of intellect, any useful foreknowledge, is created by and contains integrated Dikw; defined in a domain about a subject. Dikw is the data, information, knowledge, and wisdom (pronounced dick wa) that defines the behavior of an object under conscious consideration. These Dikw pieces multi-logically connect, creating useful new intelligence about a specific subject.

This book is an Dikw example. It takes the known data (from psychology, neurophysiology, religion, etc.), logically co-relates these observed data facts, and creates information. The in-formation describes the knowledge of how-to ideas for the materially formulation of real things; it creates content-to-context stepwise knowledge. The in-formation also, from a top-down point-of-view, frames wise decision-making. This is Dikw: Data, Information, Knowledge, and Wisdom.

My goal in writing this book is to make people (1) situation-wise, (2) behavior knowledgeable, (3) clearly in-formed, via (4) taught and learned, symbolized data facts. The book thereby contains the "Dikw" needed to communicate the who, what, why, where, when, and how of clearer thinking.

Let's take another Dikw example; the naming of this book. It was first named "Cognitive Science for Babies" and meant to be a short book that parents could read to children to put them asleep. During the process, both the parents and children learn a little Cognitive Science and would become smarter in their lifetime.

Then the publishers said, "Make it longer," and the Glossary and Examples sections were added. In completing that work and looking at the new book, it was clear that the title must be changed. A new in-context intelligence emerged, causing a behavior change. "Your Conscious brain/mind" was selected with "How to use Cognitive Science to get smarter" as its byline.

Should we keep the first title or use the second one? Once Dikw framed, once the data, information, knowledge, and wisdom points of view were overlapped, it became clear to all that it is really two useful books. Two books are what we will publish; one for babies and the other for adults. This creates more goodness and makes us more money.

HDSA/Dikw intellectual thinking is like that. If you lay out the symbols in this format, a better and more useful answer consciously arrives; it is conducted. Your individual and collective conscious ability is expanded by organizing the symbols of an issue under focus this way.

Part out the pieces, and then consciousness review to "conduct" the better answer. Doing this, using Partology, advances good thinking for all; always.

HDSA Example

A Conscious brain/mind is a unique processing tool. It is not logical. It is multi-logical. The CBM always identifies and links multiple "probable" pathways; before deciding. Each pathway is a logical point-of-view. HDSA is the base multi-logics provided by the physical Universe. It is also how a CBM works intentionally; it works symbolized ideas intelligently for its physical Life.

HDSA is an acronym that stands for linking and overlapping hierarchy, dimensionality, seriality, and alternative points-of-view. It is multi-logical; all four logics apply on each physical and conceived point simultaneously. HDSA is the framework of conscious awareness. It's how the rational conscious process operates, modeling the real world. It paints the picture. It's the holistic framework from where the creative, conducted life-improvement jumps will occur.

Think of it this way. First, focus on how the parts go into and out of the wholes. That is, name the parts and then order them into a hierarchy. This is one point-of-view. Now switch to the dimensional viewpoint to ask, "Which of these points can or must be assembled simultaneously?" This provides a different viewpoint that can improve operating efficiency. Now focus on the detailed assembly or decay by looking at the serial, stepwise processes. You are not now being strategic but tactical. Serial actions, with in-process quality checks, are very specific.

These three (HDS) are how the material Universe works. To this logical structure, now add alternatives for each point; as usefully appropriate. This is a situation-dependent, conscious judgment of part costs, tolerances, and quality. For example, if the half-inch screw falls between .489 inches and .511 inches, it can be used. Or, if the daily lunch special is $5 cheaper and the cuisine acceptable, then maybe order that. Choosing your Career Manifest Destiny is an alternative judgment that can and should be made using an HDSA/Dikw Partological evaluation.

Create an HDSA example of this for me. Take a domain of importance to you, in your current life, and first name it. Write that name or phrase in the subject field of a new email addressed to me. Next, describe the overall-life-point found in that idea domain in the first paragraph of that email. Then order and detail the Dikw defined points. Finally, overlap the HDSA multi-logics onto the Dikw points. Write these out in order.

Once done, you have written a CBM program to be called by a situation. That is partological memory, using metacognition. It's an efficient mental program that can be named, memory saved, and usefully called when needed. In this way, you-program-you to be better for <u>your</u> lifetime.

Artistic Religion is Creatively Conducted
Keep in mind that Cognitive Science is an eclectic science in that we study all intellectual fields that the Conscious brain/mind has created We look for intelligent, conscious symmetries found in all intellectual fields. By looking at philosophy, mathematics, physics, language, religion, art, etc., a Cognitive scientist can back into the mechanics of the device that created this output. Let me now define religion, as being expressed artistically, in a cinematographic work.

In 1968, Stanley Kubrick produced and directed a science fiction film titled "2001: A Space Odyssey." This was a creative, artistic work to better understand and define a lifetime religion.

The film starts with primates battling for water rights on Earth. One primate group develops tools and uses this mechanical innovation to rule supreme. That "tool use" then civilizes and advances humans into outer space, where we find and confront the monolith, representing geometrically formatted opportunity-for-life itself. Here Kubrick is describing evolution by Natural Selection in the context of a "God" provided set of geometric opportunities. It can only happen if the physical matter is to evolve (to advance geometrically) as more efficient physical forms in space over time. This future-back opportunistic force is the Deism, the Intelligent Design.

Later humans launch deep space travel to Jupiter, and we are introduced to Hal, who is a very smart and potentially selfish-aware machine. The man/machine battle ensues, with Dave, the human, winning.

The movie ends when Dave is transformed on physical death by the monolith into a fetus enclosed in a transparent orb of light floating in space above the Universe. Dave's consciousness has evolved to the level of becoming the all-seeing and all-knowing eyes of God; his conscious awareness is future affective. This is a Mormon multi-god perspective.

Is this a created work of art? Yes. Is it a religious statement? I say yes. The monolith, representing material spacetime, creates the opportunity for an all-knowing and all-seeing intentional entity, imaged as God. That is the intent of the monolith and also the intent of the Universe, so presents Stanley Kubrick. Life wants and creates more alive forms, and so it goes.

Quantum Decision-making

Quantum means "one". Max Planck used it to describe and measure how energy, in its smallest quantity, is transferred and moves. This is the Planck constant 6.62607015×10^{-34} J·Hz^{-1}. Others used this key insight to develop Quantum mechanics and Quantum Field Theory. In the same way, sensations idealize decisions in the Conscious brain/mind. Many ideas co-relate, creating one intelligent action and resolving a situation's intention for Life. Decisions are quantized for Life.

Quantum seems strange because when you "look" at a thing in its environment, it has two superposition states. Each thing is both a real particle (a part) and its continued wave of influence (the Partology). That is, each thing is solid and area influential; at the same time. You see these different states depending on how you are "looking" at that thing. Look for the part and find the part; look for its impactful change and you'll see and can measure that superimposed change.

This idea, its insight, is really not that strange. All real things assembly and decay in space over time at many points in spacetime. That thing (as it is step changing) has a name. This is the logical basis of Partology. It is "Quantum mechanics" applied to conscious decision-making. The CBM quantifies useful behaviors and renames the results. Each is a subject/object/verbal part.

We also find the same "quantum" relationship in language. Think of it this way; each thing has three parts: (1) inside the thing, (2) encasing the surface of the thing, and (3) outside the thing. These three parts situationally co-relate, creating the thing at a spacetime moment. Language uses subject (the encasing surface), objects (inside or outside), and verbs (thing a/effects). Language requires and uses subject-object-verbs to make intelligent statements. This is how language quantizes meaning by Selfishly viewing the parts individually and collectively.

So, the HDSA multi-logical arrangement of Dikw symbolizes parts-and-wholes quantized intelligence as material states (objects) and their co-related changes (verbs) as viewed by the active, intentional observer (subject). Ideas are insights-and-actions in themselves and also influential-bits making up a whole decision; the then reasoned ideal. It all depends upon how your consciousness is now intentionally viewing the sensed situation in relation to stored memory. This stored memory is bouton bits learning to fire together, creating a sense>decide>act pathway.

In short, the Conscious brain/mind is an organic Quantum computer that people use intentionally. Once you know this, you can take informed action to get smarter step-by-step and co-related symbol-by-symbol. Each person has the right one-new-idea that can and should be used to resolve their specific Life situations. A CBM quantizes that decided action; or not.

If you understand this HDSA stepwise process, people can program themselves "anew" as they desire for their lifetime. If you do not get this, then the World will program you in your life.

What is a Tesimal number?
Any new theory is logical, mathematical, and intentional. This is because logic, at its core, describes consistent increments toward a goal. Each step is numbered and measured. If you know how it works, how it changes given explicit conscious factors, then any intent can be quantized.

However, human consciousness (the source of all logical systems) must be more than logical. To create logic, you must be smarter than logic itself. In fact, the CBM is multi-logical. This means that a CBM uses multiple overlapping logics applied to each spacetime point at the same time. These are commonly called points-of-view. I created Tesimal numbers to map the views.

Take a large number like 1,000,000,000. Then logically divide that number into regions; each used to number and link one overlapping logic. By one convention, each hierarchal node can have a 10x10 dimensional matrix, with up to 990 serial steps; each with 10 alternatives. Doing this would logically create four linked number ranges, with four finite numbering ranges. It is a Combinetic math system we call a Tesimal number.

In this example, using a 10^{10} magnitude to overlap the HDSA logical points, the hierarchy and dimensional numbers are matrices and the serial and alternative numbered ranges are vector lines. Some numbers in the range are not used as points, only for relative positioning. This type of manifold is called a sparce matrix because not all numbers are used.

We are allocating 10 numbered end points for ten alternatives, 100 points for up to 100 process steps each node, a 3D dimensioned matrix of 100 points in each direction for simultaneous actions (100,000,000 number places), and the remaining number points set the hierarchy.

The image will help explain. It starts with a node hierarchy of a predefined depth and breath, then each node can grow into a dimensional space. From each of the dimensioned number points, a series of steps can them emerge, with alternatives. This is how ideas are consciously linked, are affectionally linked, into an ideafold.

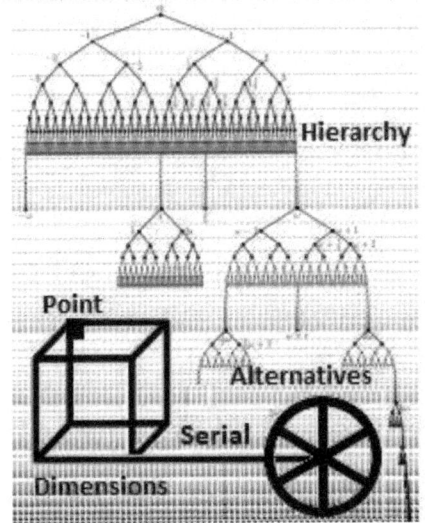

Note: A Tesimal number is finite from zero to a magnitude. The size is determined by the ranges needed to map the logic ranges. It's called a Tesimal number because it has multiple terminating points; one for each logic. Multi-logics is created by Tesimal number overlapping.

Accurate Theory Development

My theory of cognition, my description of how the CBM (Conscious brain/mind) emerged (is sustained, grows, declines, and how it works for Life) uses HDSA multi-logics to lay out the Dikw symbolism. Bouton-ideated symbols are memory pathways, properly co-related accurately or not, creating good or bad situation behaviors. My theory states, and has tested, knowing this makes a person smarter. Each person can learn it, try it, and prove this for themselves.

If you are attempting to develop a new theory, in a field of study that must be communicated and tested, then HDSA Partology can help. Here is a description of the general process.

All theories are developed in words, then logically modeled in math (or the other way around), communicated via written explanation, then tested in the real world (just follow the proposed experiment); to validate or not. You create a new theory, and test it, before you write the book.

Correct and accurate word selection is very, very important to theory development. Select the best word-set now commonly in use by your audience. Word and phrase co-relations, as it is used to describe the new theoretical subject-object-verb statements (for both communication and testing), is the crux of a new theory. You will be using HDSA and Dikw forms, that new Tesimal numbered geometry (actually it's an ideology, the linked points, placed into the HDSA Ideometry; it's a combinatorial geometry) to articulate a clear theory.

Each theory, and its co-related real-world testing instructions, form one deterministic Partology. No theory is absolute. Each is only statistically accurate in the defined domain.

So, communicate your theory to your scientific audience and let them generally comment or actually test by experiment; as feedback. Take those comments and experiment dataset examples as useful feedback and modify (1) the words and/or (2) the math co-relationship of the words to better understand and explain your new theory. All theory development is interactive. They are explained and improved by critical feedback.

If you cannot yet do that, then come up with the one phrase that defines your domain of study. That is the foundational stone on which to develop a sound theory. Each theory is always about one named thing. All other theory statements directly and efficiently support that one domain named notion.

This is an example of the Partology method of cognition, used to develop and test a theory. Intellect development is stepwise ordered via HDSA multi-logics, using Dikw symbolism. That is the point of my tested theory. Using the Partology method in other theoretical developments will be added examples of the testing of my cognitive theory.

Congruent Modular Forms

The Partological method, of conducting life everlasting from expansive individual intent and into the creative power of the Universe, is also now being examined mathematically. Using Modular forms, from Number theory, congruent and incongruent systematic methods emerge. Congruence is deduced, and incongruence is "conducted" from the Universal influences at that time and in that space as materialized.

Congruent modular forms, and the mechanical systems they define and support, are symmetric. Incongruent modular forms are not. Innovative creativity emerges in a Conscious brain/mind from the incongruence afforded in the Universe of matter evolving in space time. The CBM can think brand new. It can logically "conduct" innovative insights from the Universe itself.

Study the two images below. The one on the left contains pattern symmetries; it is congruent. The one on the right has patterns yet contains no symmetries. Left manifests a fundamental pattern that causes subsequent symmetries to emerge. It's logic can be deduced. Right lacks an overarching pattern from which symmetry can emerge. It's logic cannot be deduced, induced, or abducted. HDSA multi-logics is not symmetrical; ends come as they may; they are conducted from above. That's why it is used creatively.

Some patterns have no symmetrical visibility. The Universe is one of these patterns. The Universe has more foreknowledge than we humans. We are content in that context. That fact allows it to fundamentally create anew. Both good and bad add intelligence to humanity.

See: https://www.quantamagazine.org/long-sought-math-proof-unlocks-more-mysterious-modular-forms-20230309/ and https://en.wikipedia.org/wiki/Modular_form#

The point; the source of advancing art and religion is the Universe itself. It creates new opportunities for Life more abundant. Quiet your mind and look up to that. Then look down, into the real physical world, for the doing. That method advances any lifetime.

Life After Death

"My mother is 83 years old, and she is now afraid of death.

What do you say to people who are afraid of death?"

I was asked this question and responded as follows:

Hi Chris,

I love this question. In 1972, when I started my work to understand the Conscious brain/mind, I selected a contextual method of study. To know the smaller piece, you must understand the larger context in which the smaller piece emerges and then exists; that is both an infra- and super-structure. Look both inside-out and outside-in to better understand the life nature of things. I started with the bouton bit, then went to look at mental consciousness, and finally my plan was to study what conscious remnants could live on after physical brain/mind death; if any. So, your question is part of Cognitive Science. It is the last question of CogSci. I think about this.

Said another way, "Conscious life after physical death is the context of consciousness". It is the overall milieu of conscious awareness. It is a metaphysical place.

The short answer is that I still do not know. What I do know is that both the metaphysical and physical worlds exist. They co-relate. This fact, true by logical definition, provides some insight into the conscious life after death question. The logic goes as follows:

Meta means beside. The metaphysical exists beside the physical; it's contextual. I expand this to say "metaphysical" means the before, after, above, below the physical. This is true by logical necessity. So, the life-after-death question becomes "When the physical dissolves, does also its metaphysical dissolve?" Or said another way, "Does the metaphysical have a "meta" that is beside it? We could name this the meta-meta space and substance.

We know that all physical things have their "beside" metaphysical influence. These two a/effect each other. This is (1) the action and (2) the "spooky action at a distance" duality of Quantum mechanics.

Let's now die and leave the physical world and become the "meta-meta physical formation". Plato's forms, and/or the religious heaven (name it what you choose), is the meta-physical. What is its "beside". Does the metaphysical have a beside meta-meta? Again, I do not know but suggest.

We could say the transfer of your mindset ideas and values into another physical form might help your conscious being live on after physical brain death. This is the purpose of biographies, memorials, tombstones, and the Afterlife website software we are now discussing. They help.

However, this skirts the key point. Is there a meta-meta, a medium structure that stands naturally beside the metaphysical of our physical world? Can we humans while alive beneficially affect the structure of the meta-meta physical for the quality of our after life?

First, what would this meta-meta space be made of? Metaphysical is ideological; it is logically formed by symbol connections. Let's ask, "What is the essential form of the logically formed?" What is its point? I would answer "intent". I'm for Life; now, then, and always. That is my essential intent that flows through all I think and do. I like living better, for longer, for us all. I see how we all can do much, much better at this. Aiding that, helping to create that better life, is my intent.

So maybe the way you personally and consciously access the meta-meta is to live there. Start now, while alive. Be for life, in all forms and for all things, now and forever.

That is as far as I can see. It is the common denominator for all that I do. In this way I'm in sync with the Universe. That's good enough for me. Remember; Life advancing is the one verse of this Universe. We can all harmonize that song.

Be honest for Life; for you, me, and us all. Be for all well living things. Hope this helps. -g

My Personal Example
Just before publishing this book, I was asked to provide a personal example of HDSA/Dikw Partology; something that I need and can use HDSA/Dikw to solve. The publisher, Amazon Publishing Pro's, asked me to use Partology to solve a problem that I now have.

My current objective is to share HDSA multi-logical thinking in an understandable way so that people can use it immediately. So, I will use Partology to explain Partology; starting with an image.

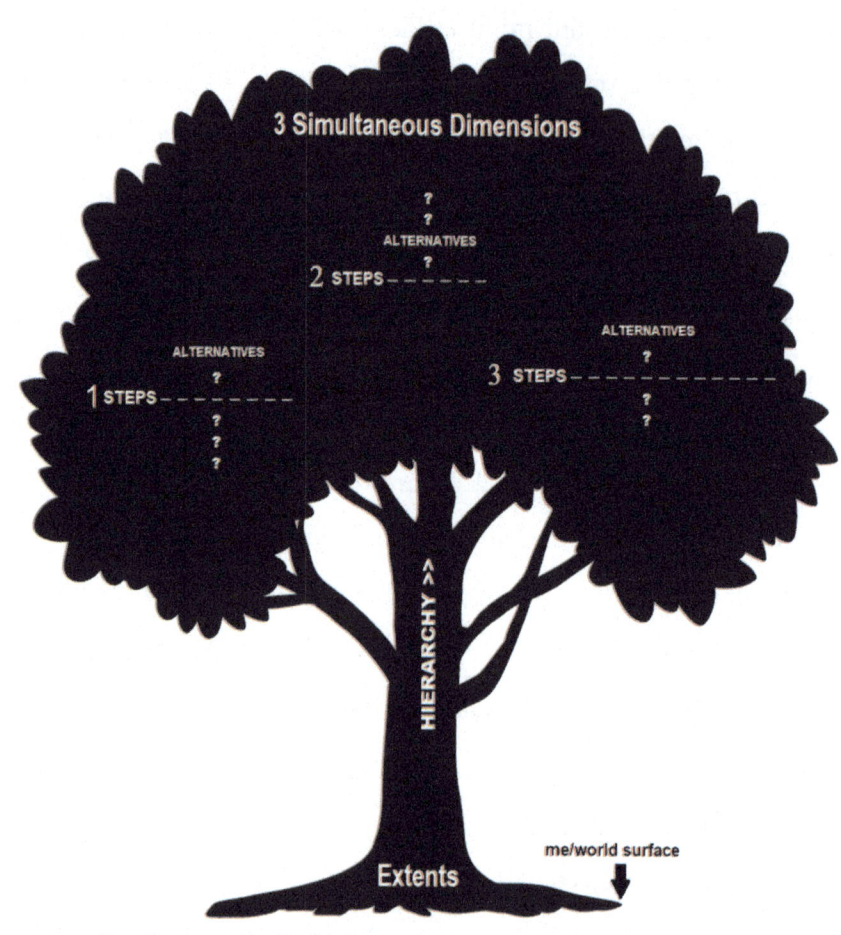

CONSCIOUS INTENTS

Here I use a tree, growing out of the ground, to illustrate the conscious surface between my intent (the roots) and the physical action that I take, the extents (the tree growth structure), to positively a/effect the world in which I live. The affect is caused by my mental intent. The effects are what I physically do to grow the influential tree; like writing this book on the CBM subject.

Both affect (probable "spooky action at a distance") and the effect (actual physical actions) influence what is to be created. Both a/effects are consciously planned and implemented. By mentally thinking it through (that internal conscious observation), without any physical action like writing and publishing this book, I influence the future world structure. Be careful of what you consciously, mentally intend. It itself is materially influential.

My ideological, actionable tree starts with one trunk, one point, that named domain (Partology is…). This starts a <u>hierarchy</u> of tree branching. It is the network of simultaneous nodes used to describe the actions that branch out into the <u>dimensions</u>.

Keep in mind that since material spacetime has many points, I can consciously plan and dimension implement multiple actions at the same time. This coordinated foreknowledge is more efficient and often essential. Many parts must be ready at the same time before the physical change.

In each dimensional point, I set up a stepwise <u>serial</u> procedure, with defined parts being connected or detached (assembly) into the more desirable whole. This is a stepwise process with <u>alternatives</u>. Those steps, dimensionally played and hierarchy organized, become the idealization.

The first three factors (HDS) exist ideally without human conscious awareness. The extended Universe itself always works with hierarchy, dimensionality, and serially overlaps. It is a live consciousness, the thing "intentional foreknowledge", that creates the alternative logic (A).

A few examples will help. I work on the "line" assembling wheels on cars. The manual says the nut ideally is .5 inches. However, I am instructed in writing that I can use nuts within the tolerance size range of .49 and .51 inches. These are acceptable options. Another example; I bought Cannabis stock and lost my shirt in their political demise. I should have kept my investment in Google; the tried-and-true growth stock. Selecting a life mate is another important social, personal, and economic decision for a lifetime; made from alternatives.

The situation intent, the collection of things and their related actions inside the "tent", creates formative objectives that then select among external alternatives. New fits are then made.

These four HDSA logics are overlapped by conscious awareness and create, in-and-from their pointed combination, various points-of-view. These are mentally examined, are consciously modeled, before a decision to act is made. The more you do this HDSA multi-logical "thinking" and re-thinking, the higher the quality of your written words and thoughts. The better life decisions that you will make. That's what I mean by HDSA/Dikw Partology makes you smarter.

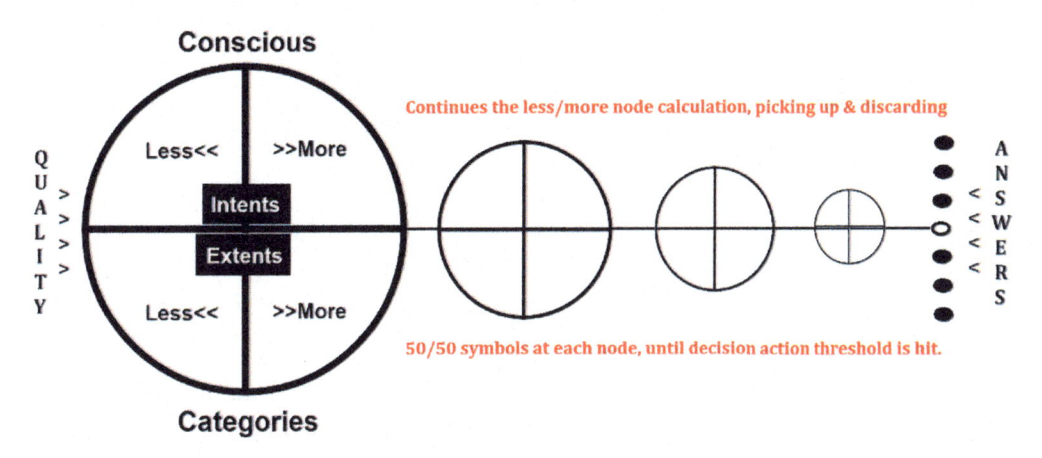

Note: Why does HDSA/Dikw Partology work? Why is it a smarter metacognition? It's how both the Universe and your Conscious brain/mind works. If your software (mind) is of a consistent form as your hardware (brain), then your consciousness is expanded. This is how it makes you smarter. It does not expand consciousness. It better uses the neurological resources that you have.

That improved utilization of your Conscious brain/mind will improve any desired composition.

Partological Composition

Many people have a difficult time writing compositions that both communicate useful information and have memorable impact; good composition motivates new and better behaviors. Partology, understanding how parts should be fitted and nestled together to create impact, can be a very useful writing tool.

Think of Venn diagrams only the meaning of the whole composition is (1) abstract filtered-down into the detail and also (2) essentially composed detail-up. The recurring theme becomes a fractal; called a dotell. Pointed, nested patterns are conducted throughout. It is a top-down, bottom-up, inside-out, and outside-in co-relation of pointed meaning; all at the same time. This is why good writing must be refined. Look at what is written and "in that context" improve it.

Take a look at the two images below. They illustrate how the ideas of a composition uses Dikw (data, information, knowledge, and wisdom) in subject-object-verb symbology. Each Dikw element is a circle enclosed, complete thought. However, they must be nested using the HDSA multi-logics for a meaningful composition that has behavior impact.

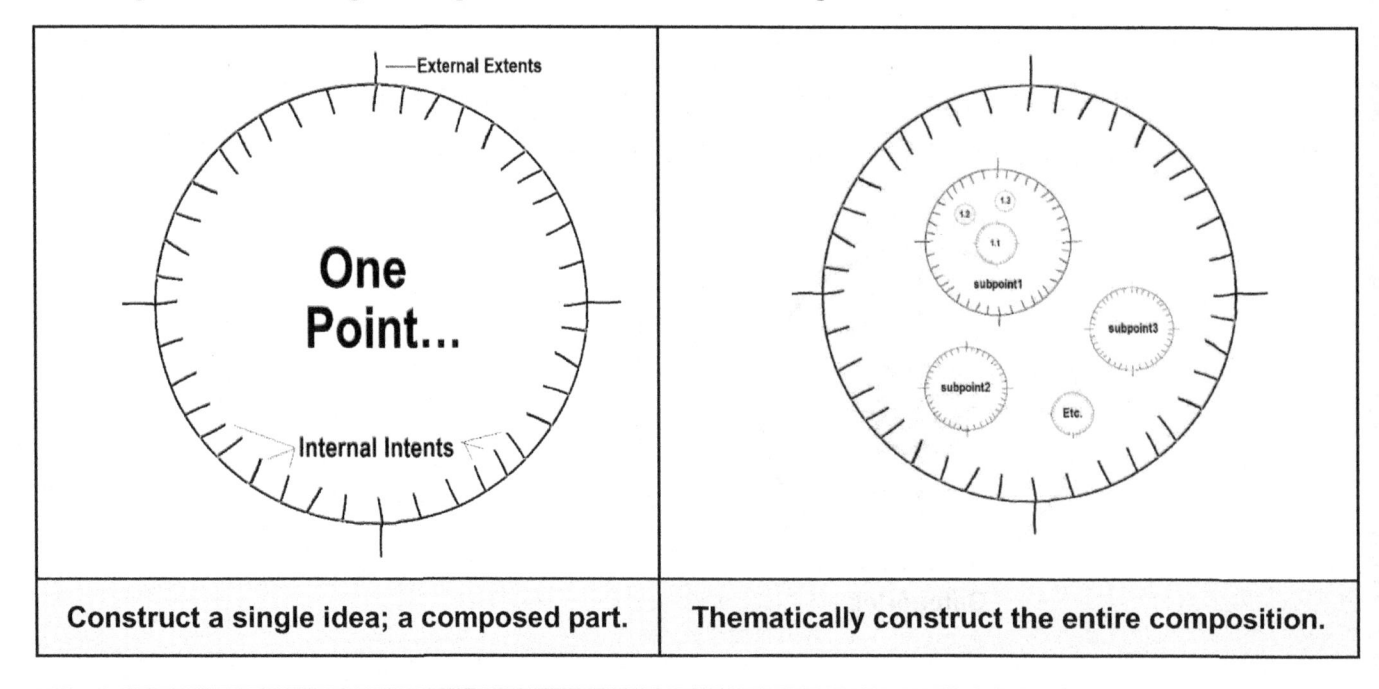

Construct a single idea; a composed part.	Thematically construct the entire composition.

The left image above illustrates one complete thought. The right illustrates how these thoughts are (1) phrase or term articulated, (2) order nested, and then (3) transitionally connected; all designed to reach the existing mindset of an audience.

The one thought is named and contains its (1) descriptive parts, (2) intents, and (3) extended connective points. The entire composition is the orderly collection of thoughts needed to make the overall point; the whole purpose of the composition. The circle represents the container of the thought and the squiggly lines are the stated or implied connections; both internally and externally. Creating powerful meaning, for an audience, requires a place for everything and all idea-termed "things" to be put into their proper place.

You outline it, write it, refine it, and then live test it; with feedback from other people. That feedback is used to create the final composition. Once done, the composition can be published for its targeted audience. In this recursive fashion, using the Partological process, your writing skills can be improved. The same idea applies to music, speeches, movies, or slide-deck creation. Any mediation can use the Partological construction methods.

The key is having new-and-useful knowledge that is well presented, in a way people can easily understand and immediately use. On your next composition, try the following steps:

1. Create the one Point, that pithy title phrase, unto which all other words will relate.
2. Then create a number of synonyms to the one point. These will be closely related terms and phrases that illuminate various roots of the one point. Each of these synonyms may become a subpoint of the overall Point. Then write about these sub-pointed synonyms.
3. Once the Point and its closely related subpoints are termed and organized into an outline, think about it again. Rephrase all points in context of all other points. Are some point superfluous; not relevant and not needed? Are their hierarchal, pointed nodes that are missing, simultaneous dimensions not covered, steps not articulated, or alternatives not identified and "in context" explained. If so, repoint by rephasing your outline. You do not want to spend time writing irrelevant materials and/or missing useful points.
4. Now write the explanations of each point. Here you can use the who, what, why, where, when, and how ideas. Keep it simple. Keep it terse. Use their language. Make it useful for your audience. Usefulness is the goal of good writing; both fiction and non-fiction.

5. After each subpoint you can place illustrative examples and offer exercises or write these in a section of their own. First make your point. Then example your point. Then have the reader use your new knowledge, point-by-point, so it mentally sticks. You will want your new ideas to have a useful, long-lasting impact upon the memory and behavior of the readers. Applied example and relevant (to the reader) exercises will help to make your knowledge understandable and remembered.

6. Do not forget to include a Glossary that clearly defines the important terms that you are using. Also, credit other people on whom you have built your new knowledge.

7. Finally, plan a follow-on transaction with your audience. You will want to develop feedback cycles with the people you serve. It could be a next book, newsletter, blog, Facebook site, YouTube video, or a monthly Podcast. In this book we offer a course (www.CogSci101.com) and the association membership (www.Metacognitions.org) as additional Cognitive Science resources to our specific audiences.

That's it. The above explains how to use Partological multi-logics in both thinking about and writing a composition of any size; from a small note to a big book. We all, always, should be improving our thinking and writing skills. If you know how your Conscious brain/mind works, linking symbolized parts via HDSA/Dikw, you can make it work better. That is my one Point.

Academic feedback

A number of university professors have been providing useful feedback on Partology; this HDSA multi-logical method of associating Dikw symbols for Life. For example:

"Gary, as I read your book I kept wondering why you do not use the term non-linear?" HDSA is not non-linear. In fact, the S is serially linear. Plus, each logic overlapped can be serially numbered. The whole of the HDSA numbering schema contains multiple terminating serial arrays. This is why that numbering method is called a combinatorial "Tesimal"; it has multiple terminations. The HDSA math system has four linear numbers; it is multi-linear.

"Your work is more like an outline of an entire philosophy of mind, and as such touches on an extensive range of issues and associated literatures; a comprehensive, responsible critique would itself have to be book-length." To understand how the Conscious brain/mind works, I needed to look at everything that Consciousness has created (math, language, art, religion, business, politics, etc.), to find the common denominator, and then link those common parts together. Once done, it is now simple. Your Conscious brain/mind multi-logically symbolizes

reality and bouton stores those patterns in memory, as connected pathways. If you know this "you can symbol program you" to be smarter. A lot of study condenses to this one HDSA/Dikw point.

"As a logician, this 'conduction' intrigues me." Heretofore the Self has been stated as the "hard problem of Consciousness". More essential is creativity. How does a personal Self, create insight anew. A new creation cannot be generated by deduction, induction, and/or abduction; true new comes from elsewhere. There must be another logical force and method at work. It turns out that the human mind is much smaller than the Universe. We can therefore not "know it all". So, the Universe offers new insights, new situational pattern of life and death decisions. The CBM in humans can creatively "conduct" that new insight into our conscious being. It's down felt.

"At first I did not like adding an 's' to logic. Now I ask, "Why only four linked logics?" In looking at the Universe we see Hierarchy, Dimensionality, and Serial logics at work; at the same time. These emerge from Euclidean geometry and the Cartesian framework. Einstein "curved" these but still kept the local, incremental measurements of 4D spacetime. Quantum mechanics added the measurable impact of observation. The things outside the thing, beyond the surface of the thing, affects both the measurement and future composition of the thing under consideration. There are four HDSA overlapping logics in Conscious mechanics; including Alternative selection.

"I am an expert at neurophysiology and can say that nobody knows how the human mind works. Cajal's work, the bouton claim, is very old and has been discredited. For you to claim otherwise is a falsehood." My suggestion is to read this book carefully and ask a specific question. Plus, if you want, I will teach you how to think using HDSA multi-logics. When/if it makes you smarter; that is the personal proof you need.

"Are you implying that the quantal interpretation of bouton "behavior" is purely based on the probabilistic nature of vesicle "release" (i.e., fusion with the membrane, thus releasing neurotransmitter at the fusion site)" Or, is your employment of quantum refer to the scale/resolution of the underlying processes (whatever they may be)?" Each bouton individually fires-or-holds (1) being "push" by the built-up sensation energy in their neuron and (2) then pulled by the previously developed bouton pathways. The "pull" is future-back from upstream and the "push" is past-forward from downstream. Boutons hold below their Action potential and release once that threshold is reached. They grow foreknowledge by their change in synaptic conductivity.

"Yesterday, I had a very nice conversation with a contemporary Cognitive Scientist and he brought up *Augustine's "City of God" metaphor."* This was not discussed in a Catholic religious sense. Instead, we talked about this idea from a CogSci perspective; from a provable, scientific perspective.

The ideas went as follows: (1) the purpose of life is to live well, for as long as you can, (2) this is an intellectual process; via scientific feedback, we all learn from mistakes, (3) nobody is now perfectly ideal, therefore, (4) life is a journey of experiencing, understanding and remembering how to live better. Then we added Augustine's idea of a city. No person is an island. We all are, and best operate, in a civilized society.

Universal love

A while back I overheard a young child on the phone, with his mother who was away, saying "When it gets dark a family should all be together." The mother responded with love.

Why is love the strongest idea, emotion, and action found in the Universe? Because it physically aligns the intents of multiple objects. That formation both creates and promotes Life.

More love is better. Less hate is better. Indifference to evil is also a deadly behavior. Be wise in consciously choosing what you love, hate, and where you are indifferent.

The purpose of Evil

In a Cognitive Science class, I was asked about evil. This is always a good question but might be especially relevant today. Look around. Either the world is eviler today or the same level of evil behaviors are being better web-reported.

Why is their evil. The answer is that it's a cognitive, logical necessity. There is no good without evil; a vector has two ends. Evil is a relative term; one end of the measurement stick.

.

Good <<<<<<<< >>>>>>>> **Evil**

How would you know what is good without knowing what is bad? Cognition is symbolically both measured and relative. Evil is <u>not</u> good for Life. The purpose of Evil is to define and implement deadly behaviors. The lack of evil is the good thing.

Do not be afraid of Evil. Do not run from it. Instead know, measure, and manage Evil. Let it show you its inverse, that more Life way, and then head in that direction. Good is always for life.

Friedrich Nietzsche was a genius. He understood that humanity must get beyond modern Christian Church doctrines to advance Our Kind. He, and others, broke humanity from the idea clutches of "Churches". This break was his first planned step.

However, even with searching his entire life, he never found the next-step-idealization that would take us forward. He could not replace the idea of God; try as he did. That search drove him mad. Nietzsche tried a few ideas but was never successful in finding the ideological cornerstone for Life. View a few YouTube videos on Nietzsche's unresolved search.

Part of what we are attempting to do in Cognitive Science is to link physics with metaphysics into one co-related, fundamental idealization for all of humanity. This is no small task. It is also fraught with many possible mistakes. You can reference how Hitler used Nietzsche's ideas of "Superhuman", "Master race", and "The Will to Power" improperly; in Hitler's "Triumph of the Will" ideas and the starting of WW2.

To do this, to find and cogently idealize the one overall point of any mental hierarchy (that context at the most top level, for us all), we must find the "cornerstone" of (1) all thought, (2) conscious awareness, and (3) the purpose of the Universe itself. This might not exist and it is very dangerous to try; but try we must!

Herein I say "Life", for all, lived more abundantly. I say that advancing Life is the recuring underlying point of the Universe. This is Jesus' idea. He was not for churches. Instead, he recommended that all people quiet their mind and talk to God; the Creator of the Universe. Do this daily to live better. That works for me. Remember, God is good-for-life by definition.

Where does God fit?

All things are created from parts; are caused by some named thing. By definition, what created the "Heavens and the Earth" we humans call God. God, the word, is a tautology. God is true by definition. If you like, you may use the word Good for God; they are synonyms. Note: You can define and use a synonym for the word God. Just let people know. Here I use Good to mean God.

This Good might be an "I Am" fulfilled. However, people are not born complete. Better is "we are" what we make of ourselves. There is a responsibility to use time and resources wisely for your life and the life of us all. It comes with Life. Good Life is an economist. It seeks efficient, life-providing behavior. Better is naturally selected to advance. Life comes with a continuous test.

Human Life is essentially an Opportunity to become more alive. Each person can learn how to live better, for longer, on less. Good conscious awareness knows, and teaches, how to do that.

HDSA/Dikw Partology is metacognition that advances a person's conscious lifetime. It makes you more good, better, more alive. There are fewer questions and more answers. You get smarter. Thereby our lives, in the community of humans, collectively advance.

You will find that every good thought you have follows the HDSA/Dikw logical method. Above, we describe via examples: Teaching Smarter, Practical Partology, Commonwealth errors, Career Manifest Destiny, personalizing Public schools, finding the right mate, resolving Trumpism with quality leadership, affective words, a time-efficient ideology, smarter generations, judging uncertainty, eating an elephant, Deinians, getting more impact, size of Consciousness, the recursive and universal "bouton", Dikw, Partology poetry, artistic religion, Quantum decision making, accurate theory development, congruent math forms, life after death, knowledge trees, academic feedback, loving behaviors, Evil's role in cognition, the word God (God is Good), and now you are creating a practical example of your HDSA/Dikw multi-logical thinking for me.

Email it to me GaryDeines@Boutonics.com and my people will grade your conscious work and return our evaluations. Those personal examples are the best way to learn how to make your Conscious brain/mind work better. The more you think in HDSA/Dikw Partology terminology (the more you use this Deinian manifold method), the smarter you will become. Let us know how it works, or does not work, for you. We can answer most questions.

Author Note

Learning how your Conscious brain/mind works is a new task. You learn it bit-by-bit, word by word, concept by concept. With each term, you must "think about it". Then you must apply it.

For example, your "Conscious brain/mind" is a term (CBM); what does that mean? What does CBM refer to, and is it important to think about that thing? Is hardware, software, and intent-ware a good synonym for the three layers of a CBM. Some will say no! Leave me alone to be who I am. Others will say, go ahead, help make me smarter for my lifetime. You can directly program you.

Is the idea of thinking in the HDSA/Dikw Partology method, the creating and using named SIPO (Situation Input>Process>Output) Deinians, mentally powerful? Why do this? Think about it and then try it. See if it makes you smarter.

How is a "dotell" like a fractal? How does it sum up the information essentially in a pithy phrase. Why does the detail and its dotell summary aid understanding and memory. Please use the glossary to look-up the definition of a "dotell phrasing."

To get smarter, start using the HDSA/Dikw Partology methodology. It's metacognition that works because it is how the Universe works essentially for Life, advancing lifetimes.

Let us know how it works for you. In fact, post a review at a website for others to read. Get the word out. The entire World needs to become a whole lot smarter, and a bit more moral, for us to collectively move forward into a better Life for you, me, and us all.

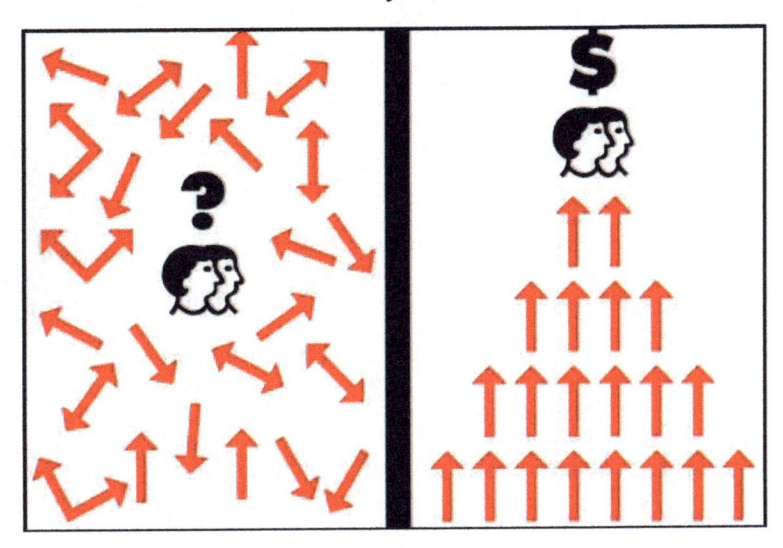

The more you align your ideas into the HDSA/Dikw Partology, the better life becomes.

Glossary of Cognitive Science Terms

This is a glossary to define the terms that co-relate into this theory. It is used to prove the ascertains and for publishing results. Making people smarter is how we prove the veracity of the ideas and multi-logical methods contained herein.

The knowledge contained in this book is called metacognition. It is thinking about how you think, so that you can learn to think better. As such, each term is positioned to connect and overlap.

Each idea, each symbolized word or phrase, represents one piece of the whole. Each term makes you a bit smarter. Once you have understood all words and phrases, and know how they co-relate, your Intelligence Quotient will increase and your Life will improve.

Why does this happen? It's because you start using consciousness the way that the Conscious brain/mind works. Therefore, you are not battling the basic ideological structure in the Universe or your Conscious brain/mind. Instead, you know and understand Partology; that HDSA/Dikw multi-logical method of ideally co-relating symbols for Life insights and behaviors.

A/effects, a new term, quantize the effects (past forward) and affects (future back) simultaneously. Please note that the evolution of all things, including new ideas, are pushed and pulled into being. Sometimes the extents (things outside the thing) are in control. At other times the intents (things inside a thing) are in control. At all times both the extents and intents co-relate a/effectively to create the outcome. A/effect is the cause of the "many-many body" problem; the cause of mental complexity and the source of creativity.

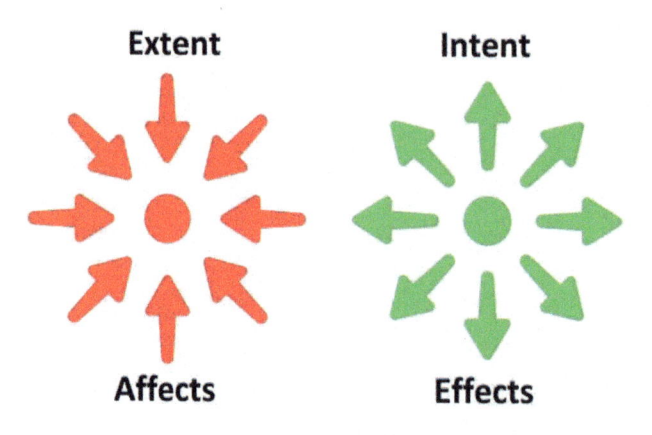

ACE is an acronym for the Afferent >> Cognitive >> Efferent neuronal structures that are located in the Peripheral (PNS) and Central Nervous Systems (CNS).

Actualized means becoming your best manifest destiny. The current ideological formation of each individual will point to a life work that is ideal. Actualization, via informed trial and error, finds that ideal way for each person.

Affects are future-back forces. They come from the universal opportunities for Life; as then formatively expressed. Lifetime insights are "conducted" into understanding, are creatively read and pieced together consciously, before behavior improvement. Conscious things are affected by these Life opportunities. They then act out the effects; for the results.

Affect Causes the Effect (another ACE). Cause and Effect is insufficient to describe the change that occurs in both the real and ideological worlds. This is because affect causes the effect based upon the Life opportunity to do so. Affects are selected; both inside-out (life of thing) and outside-in (Universal Life). The Cause-and-Effect thinking must be upgraded to "Affect Causes Effect".

Agency is the essential function of a Conscious brain/mind (CBM). The CBM agencies, as manifested by bouton sets, create your conscious Self.

AIRIGI stands for the integration of AI (Artificial Intelligence), RI (Real Intelligence) and GI (Good Intent). The appropriate linking of these three perspectives is the best mental model we have for developing future systems. This is the new way, a less chauvinistic way, of stating the useful, man/machine interface. Start with good intent, add AI, then interface human RI for Life.

Alternatives is a logical method defining one of the available possibilities. It's the A part of HDSA multi-logics. Options are normally ranked for fitness, and potential reward, given a then in-context ideal formation for your and our life.

Artropy, a new term, is the in-formed process of part assembly; as intended for Life by a conscious thing. It, that artropic assembly, is the inverse of entropic decay. It assembles more efficient living life forms. Artropy is a statistical measure of part connection assembly and an indication of the intentional action needed to increase that behavior probability. Artropy mathematically co-relates content in context, as intended.

Assembly adds a part or energy quanta to a whole. Decay removes a part from a whole. Life is opportunistically, artistically assembled; and then it decays. It's a recursive process from simple to multi-logically complex.

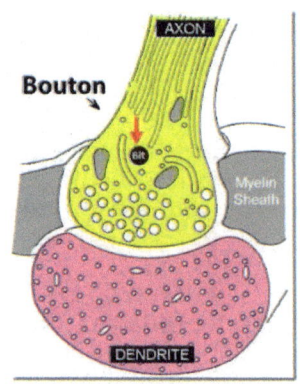

Bouton (button) is an axon growth, into the neuron synapse, that fires action potential, or not. Boutons are the neuronal pathway "bits" that make up, that symbolize, situation ideas and ideals. Each bouton is a quantum bit and also a Quantum computer; they compute relative firing rates. Boutons learn from aware experiences as influenced by each other. Conscious mechanics, the step beyond Quantum mechanics, mathematically co-relates bouton firing; predicting and creating conscious awareness. Cajal first imaged boutons and shared the 1906 Nobel Prize in medicine for so doing. Please note that the word "bouton" is like the word "atom". Neither are real but are scalable idealizations. They are contextual thought-tools at any level of gradation. Bouton, button, is a very useful word is that it can encompass the smallest real thing and the largest real thing; both placed in the context that created and supports that thing.

Brain is physical. Brain is the physical neurons that are distributed into an Afferent (sensation in), Cognitive (decision making), and Efferent (instruction out) system: ACE. The Conscious brain/mind makes a decision and mind recursively, spirally, remembers to learn from the results of these decisions.

Career Manifest Destiny (CMD) is derived from your existing bouton set; as intentionally modifiable by Self; in that situation. Each individual has a most probable Career Manifest Destiny. Finding it advances your lifetime. You then make more money per hours doing what you love.

Causal sign is < for assembly and > for decay. < means to make; it's constructive. > means to break; it's destructive. These are final causal signs in a recursive causation (not an equation). Multiple <<< or >>> indicate nested levels of subassembly. Consciousness is not equal (=). Instead, it is intentionally causal <> in representation by situation decisions and actions. Universal, conscious awareness "causes" future materializations

Causality is the set of opportunistic factors-and-things that create a different physicality in the future. It is always by situation. In space over time material reformulates. That reformulation is "caused" by a set of factors. The predictive mathematics which describes causality is called a Causation. It is HDSA/Dikw Tesimal numbered.

CBM is an abbreviation for Conscious brain/mind.

Central Nervous System (CNS) is a decision organ, a biological computer, composed of bouton connected neurons, creating symbolized behavior pathways, housed in the cranium.

Change happens. Both things and the ideas that represent things can evolve from less complex onto more connected and complex Life thought-forms. Each thing, and its associated thought, is held together for a while and then decay from complex to their simpler parts and the ideal connections of those parts. Both ideas and things evolve intentionally.

Civil means well-breed, by a community, for individual and collective life. Boutons are civilized by other boutons. Humans are culturalized and civilized by the just behaviors found, learned and meme remembered in communities of humans.

Cognition is the mental process and result of acquiring HDSA co-related Dikw (data, information, knowledge of wisdom) about an intentional subject of interest. Cognition is a situation formative process, creating decisions of value to a lifetime.

Cognitive Science (CogSci) researches the structural nature of ideas as they affect the behavior of a Conscious brain/mind and its impact upon material bodies. CogSci uses the Scientific method of hypothesis, theory, mathematics, physical testing, and publishing results for peer review. The goal of CogSci is to create meta-knowledge and metacognition; to develop generalized mental insights that people may use to improve both their and our collective lifetimes. Making people smarter for Life in general and their life in particular; this is the single goal of Cognitive Science.

Cognitive testing: Cognitive Science is a Social Science; we describe how sensations a/effect mental structures into probable human behaviors. The resultant measure is always a statistic, as a percentage, taken and measured in-vivo, "in life". We statistically measure how people respond to new ideas; those cogs in their context.

Compromise for our lifetimes. Boutons compromise their directional polarity for their lifetime. They get in step with the collective Life opportunities of all other boutons. So should we humans. If you properly give up a little, over time, you will develop more productive relationships with other people that are more efficient for all lifetimes. Think about when and how to compromise. Individually and collectively flow with "Old man river" and not selfishly against it.

Conscious brain/mind (CBM) is an organ that intentionally processes co-related symbols to know, remember, predict, and act for its life duration, quantity, and quality.

Conscious mechanics (CM) is a step beyond Quantum mechanics. It intentionally quantizes sensations into judgments that result in specific mental and life behavior connectives. "No action" is an action. CM uses similar mathematical methods to Quantum mechanics, to quantize connective actions, only there are two calculations; one for past forward effect (bottom-up) and the second for forward back affect (top-down). Context is morphologically affected by intention. The a/effect, push/pull calculations apply simultaneously to each part, in the Partology, as intentionally desired and objectively judged by a Conscious brain/mind. The CM calculations are "causations" that follow Tesimal numbering formats in defining the "recipe" for life more abundant; for that Self, in their current situation. Conscious mechanics discretely calculates, understands, and predicts part connections and disconnections states and activities. Each of these events has an economic calculation (not a tensor), performed by the individual, in that situation.

Consciousness is metaphysical; it is aware of co-related symbols as carried upon electromagnetic waves. Consciousness is intentional; it calculates and decides for the life of things. Consciousness is the sixth sense. It is bouton-firing structures being subjectively aware of other bouton structures. Conscious awareness is "conducted" from the Opportunity for life (Op) provided by the Universe.

Conduction is a newly defined logical structure. It is beyond the deduction (within), induction (towards), and abduction (away) logical methods. Life is the skewing point; it is artfully conned into being until decay; those smaller pieces awaiting their next "con" duction. Life advancement is "conducted" into existence by the living things; as then judged and acted upon. Life is a spiral, a stairway, a stepped process up. What cons material life to advance? The Opportunity for life to be more abundant is the opening upwards. Conduction logically uses, communicates, least-energy ways and means. It seeks more for less. That opportunity is materially conducted to advance Life.

Con-duction, conduction, is different from induction. The human being is not inducing new insight, is not finding the essence of a new set of things from the existing known things. Rather, a thing smarter than we, the Universe itself, is conning us into creatively seeing a new and better Life way. You develop ideas to look up. In this forceful way, new and more intelligent life methods come into human beings. Life's reasons guide that way up, by situation, as appropriate for us all.

Conscious computer is an intentional computer that uses a particle/wave, future/back, situational Input/Process/Output (SIPO) sensing, deciding, and acting device to compute for a Life reason. A Conscious computer's memory structure is a many-many-body structure, quantized as steps on and in a stage. Each step, in each context, a/effects all other memory recorded steps. Each step looks for "best actions" given both the current extents and the Self willfully selected intents. Conscious computers co-relate symbols in action; as memory named and probably weighted. The situational algorithm is selected and placed to recursive read the framed Deinian, until the best answer is numerically derived. The best answer maximizes Life-for-the-thing(s) while minimizing energy use, effort, and risk. Life is Self-affected. Until machines can sense Life Opportunity directly, Conscious computers will need to be operationally assisted by humans. See AIRIGI.

Content is information inside a context. All in-formation is known, is creatively conducted, understood, and judged as co-related content inside an intentional context. For meaning to be made, content always exists inside a context.

Context is information that surrounds the content. It's the extent; the recurring x-formations outside the thing. Content-in-context is a recursive process from the smallest individual quanta to the one Universe; each a stepped bouton (an intentionally quantized button). Real things and the ideas that model the existence and movement of real things are contextual, HDSA recursions. This is Partology; parts into wholes. It is a method of modeling the idealized behavior of real things.

Context of Consciousness is Opportunity. Consciousness is <u>not</u> based upon the quantized Standard Model of subatomic particles (as they wave into and out of existence, based on their half-life). Nor is it based upon the physical $E=MC^2$ being affected by the gravitational curvature of space-time at the Cosmological point-of-view. Consciousness is not equal to things; it is creative, it's newly causal. The continuing and expanding Opportunity for the intentional reformation of matter is constantly provided by the Universe anew; as a fixed amount of energy/matter is reformed; in an ever-expanding spacetime. Opportunity for Life more abundant is the one verse of this Universe. We're now conscious of that fact. We individually and collectively can channel that.

Co-relate theory: Any new theory starts with defining the terms. These will be subjects, objects, and verbs. Then it logically co-relates the terms, via spacetime behavior, into a provable or unprovable theoretical ascertain, to be materially tested. No theory is absolute; they are probable.

Co-relations are the verbs. They are how general thoughts and specifically intended ideas are affected by and effect real physical behaviors; a/effect is one of many ideological co-relationships.

Cranium is the skull, especially the part enclosing the CNS (Central Nervous System).

Datum is one fact about an object. Data, many datum points, factually describes things in process (situational outcomes) using probabilities, as statistically measured. Data is part of the Dikw quad.

Decay subtracts a part from a whole; described at any mass or energy level. Assembly adds a part or energy to a whole. Lifeforms, those consciously alive entities, decay in space over time and then their parts may re-assemble intentionally, elsewhere.

Deinian is a quantized measurable manifold of a/effective points as Tesimal numbered. It is an intentionally related set of ideas. The impact due to any one point (particle or idea) will vary due to the impact of all the other idealized points in the whole system. Deinians are ideological Hamiltonians; the first is for modeling consciously connected ideas and the second for modeling system defined particles. Where Hamiltonians measure the total physical energy in a defined system, Deinians use Tesimal numbering to account and measure the Life providing Opportunity of a domain of intelligence, as it situationally relates to a Self. Deinians mathematically model the many-many body problem of current intents a/effecting < > the short- and long-term extents.

Think of a Deinian as a multi-logical subset of Hamilton's idea. It is a generalization of the concept of a connected space into a HDSA formatted structure. As such, it tersely models Point of View consciousness. In limiting the Hamiltonian, via Deinian situation focus, improved decisions can be made, followed by more efficient action.

Dikw is an abbreviation indicating four types of linked and ordered symbolism: data, information, knowledge, and wisdom. Data is a fact. Information logically co-related facts. Knowledge is know-how and Wisdom is knowing when to apply what knowledge. Information is more important than a datum, knowledge more important that information, and wisdom is the most life important of all.

Dimensionality, provided by the Universe, is understood as both a physicality and a logical method. It's the order and measure of simultaneous spatial point/events in the HDSA multi-logical frame. Each point/event is a hierarchal node, dimensionally modeled, and serially acted, using the best alternatives for your, mine, and our lifetimes.

Dotell, a new word, is like a fractal. It is the overlapping, formulaic meaning between hierarchal sets. Dotell phrases can be used to sum-up larger bodies of points. As such, they are a memory aid for linking details. Hardware, software, and intent-ware is a dotell for the Conscious brain/mind.

Duality of brain/mind describes how all physical things are both (1) an ideology and how each idea has (2) its physicality. Consciousness adds <u>intent</u>, that alternative selection process, creating a trinity (see AIRIGI). It is a Conscious brain/mind triumphant. Bits, boutons, and idea symbols are in-context, on/off (plus minus), part/whole representations; intentionally symbolized into an ideological manifold. This situation framed manifold, called an "ideafold" or a Deinian, is consciously representing specifically defined situations and options, creating the relative positioning where ideas can be part numbered, measured, linked, and judged; assembled like a recipe. The Conscious brain/mind triumphant is not AI. It is Real Intelligence (RI).

Effects are past-forward forces. Affects are future-back forces. Life opportunities are found in between these two competing forces.

Enveloping is the process of a contextual surface surrounding a set of parts to create a new whole. This is both a physical and ideological phenomenon; beginning with protein folding. Partology is an intentional envelopment used to recursively create consciousness. Partology, a Self-agency causation, sets and remembers the internal enveloped content, in its named context, as situationally intended, remembered, and used.

Entropy is the natural process of how parts decay over time. Parts lose their connections based on half-life calculations. Artropy is the inverse. It defines how parts intentionally assemble. Both are universal competing forces, based on the strength of the then internal and external intention.

Evolution is a Life process of assembly and decay. Energy waves into matter and out again. It does so based upon a structural, Universal opportunity for Life more abundant. Life advancing is the intention of the Universe. As co-related energy waves of specific spectral frequencies overlap, evolve into, explicit spacetime points, that energy will materialize into matter; into particles. This explicit particularization holds for a period of time and then energy waves, of same or different spectral frequencies, decay from that pointed matter via the $E=MC^2$ formulation. Note: Partology is a structured thinking method that multi-logically maps the evolution of all energy waves, or particles, assembling into and out of named parts of a consciously intended whole. Partology HDSA/Dikw maps that event chunked, piecemeal process both ways; assembly and decay.

Extension is the tension between the relevant parts outside a thing. As such it is relative. The extents ideologically co-relate with the consciously selected intentions, causing a probable result.

Foreknowledge is knowledge in advance of its becoming. Knowledge, know how, and Wisdom, know when; are both types of foreknowledge. Data and Information are "past" knowledge, they are historical, they describe what has actually happened in the past.

Formation is generative for the life or death of a thing; both by universal design and conscious selection. Conscious insights and behaviors individually and collectively create future formations; those new states. An intentional mind is over matter. We humans collectively form the future.

Gene is a DNA defined pattern of behavior, naturally selected over time for life qualities. Genes are physical. Memes are culturally selected-and-maintained ideological insights for life of individuals and communities. Both genes and memes pass life intelligence to future generations.

HDSA is an abbreviation for the Hierarchy, Dimensionality, Seriality, with Alternatives; it is a multi-logics. It links by overlapping these four logics; creating intended-stepped-parallel operations with selected alternatives. HDSA is the multi-logical bases of conscious awareness.

Hierarchy is a logical method. It is the arrangement and classification of things according to relative importance, order, or inclusiveness. It space-timely outlines how matter parts can and will go into and out of wholes. An outline, taxonomy, and/or Venn diagram use hierarchal logic.

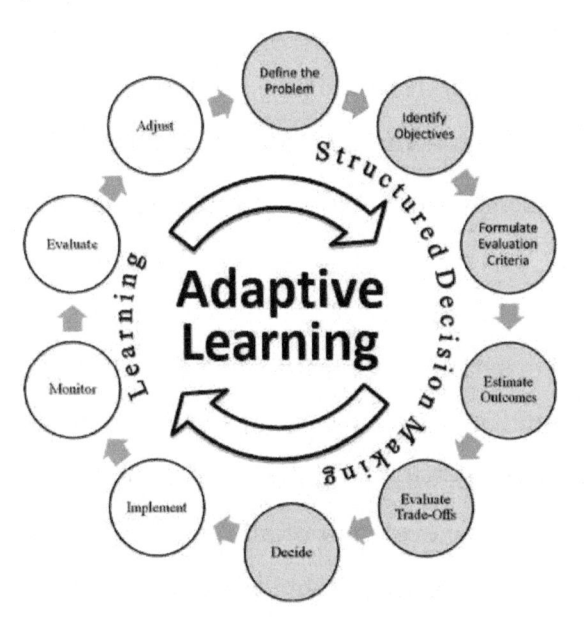

Ideas are situation specific intents to think about, reason, and act one way over another. **Ideals** are the best "idea" given a current intent and the current life opportunity provided by the extents. The CBM calculates ideal behaviors from adaptive algorithms stored in the named situation idealized memory.

Ideafold is a recurring part-into-whole, situation intention, math framed, & symbol named manifold. Memory is an ideafold of taught/learned life intents. Ideafolds are not fields but recipes. They are recipes of multiple part/fields using a Combinatorial math.

Ideology is often a misunderstood word. Ideologies can be good for life, or not. The word means the logic (logy) that connects your ideas. Each ideology is situation dependent. All are idea level nested. A mindset is made up of situation dependent, nested ideologies. These are meaningfully linked symbols. HDSA, using Dikw symbology, is a multilogical ideology for creating and remembering ideological sets. This means HDSA is a metacognition. It is smart about smartness.

Ideometry is idea geometry. It is an intentional field where symbolized ideas are linked to purposely achieve a stated objective; given a current situation and a consciously judged intent. The

76 Your Conscious brain/mind

Conscious brain/mind uses idiomatic measures to order and probably judge desired outcomes, in advance of action. The elements of an Ideometry are not converted equally. Rather, the functions are materially causal. Equations do not represent ideologies. Creative causations do.

Information is the logical correlation of data inside the thing. In-formation (another term for information) physically in-forms it. Information is part of Dikw.

Intention is the relevant tension between the parts inside-a-thing. It co-relates with Extensions, parts outside the thing, helping to cause a result. What is the named situation, its intentions, and the various named extents? Both a/e forces are known and reviewed by the Conscious brain/mind.

Intentionality is like geometry. It is a general field of study (an idea field of play) that has its points, serial lines, parallel planes, and three-dimensional hierarchical mechanics. However, Intentionality is not evaluated in a consistent, square spacetime. Instead, it accounts for part assembly/decay steps, mapped as symbols, placed into a known recipe for a more abundant, intended lifetime. A measured, intentional unit is an orderly action and not a point in spacetime.

Inverted consciousness. Structurally, mechanically, consciousness is a co-related inversion. It is a connected, intended point re-viewing process of inside-out and outside-in; where both are a/effective (a/e). When the external forces become critical, as sensed, the out-side is in conscious review; to then become understood by in-side contemplation. When inside thoughts prevail, an intentional decision is made, that is then manifested by an out-side factoring and judged action package. Conscious waves do not collapse. They invertedly iterate in/out, point by point, to arrive at the more intelligent judgment. In this way, "what is" can intentionally be made better by this iterative, inverted conscious reasoning. In-out>> Out-in>> In-out>> Out-in>> etc. to a decision.

Judge and Do (JAD) is the process a Conscious brain/mind does in sensing, deciding, and acting for its intentional lifetime. These JADs can factor both short- and long-term economic benefits. Given a sensed situation, and the CBM currently wants so-and-so, then implement this know-how. That process is a wise judgment, leading to a reasoned action, for Life more abundant.

Judging is one thing intentionally selecting among a group of other things. These can be parts, ideas, terms, behaviors, pathways, etc. You consciously judge by selecting a neuronal pathway, set in boutons, from the known and remembered alternatives. Consciousness co-relates the relevant situational factors, using HDSA/Dikw symbolism stored upon synchronized bouton firings, as intended for Life more abundant. Consciousness judges for Life; yours, mind, and ours.

Knowledge is procedurally stepped know-how. It's the how-to assemble and/or disassemble any real thing. Knowledge is part of Dikw. It knows about, has mentally documented, the more efficient assembly and decay processes of each named thing.

Life is the intentional and joyful animation of matter. It is the condition that distinguishes organic from inorganic matter. Life includes the capacity for Self-awareness, growth, reproduction, adaptive actions, and a continual change preceding death. Life is the overall universal point. Living things take action to promote more life. Life is the one verse of the Universe. Advancing Life is the recurring endpoint. We think to live. Cognitive Science is a Life Science.

Life more abundant is an opportunity recursively created by and supported by the Universe itself. The CBM senses and channels new and better Life times. These innovative lifeforms are not deduced or induced; rather they are logically "conducted" as newly created situational forms; selected for both their advanced physical and ideological lifetime qualities.

Logic is a specific system, a set of principles underlying the arrangements of elements. There are many logical forms like hierarchy, dimensions, serial, alternative, syllogisms, deductive, inductive, conductive, etc. Logics are reasoned. Each logic, including all multi-logics, employs one unique incremental numbering method. A specific mathematical numbering symbolism underlies each and all single or multi-logics.

Logics, with an "s", is the collection of simultaneous logical methods now being applied to material parts at the same spacetime. Logics create and direct multiple conscious points-of-views into a subject matter. Logics are multi-logical. A CBM uses multiple simultaneous overlapping logics to symbolize the sense, judgment, and action of intellect. HDSA is a multi-logics.

Many-many body problem of the Conscious brain/mind co-relates the current <u>intent</u> a/effecting <=> the short- and long-term <u>extents</u>. The many-many body problem extends the "many-body problem" of physics into the domain of conscious awareness. Real intelligence, RI not AI, uses Partological probabilities to approximate best-guess answers to the situational opportunity for Life more abundant. A CBM resolves the many-many body problem intuitively, symbolically, via conducting opportunities for Self lifetimes. One "many" is what I've physically got. The next "many" is what I want, given the current Opportunity. In that a/effect co-relationship, the best answer is found. A Conscious brain/mind names it, frames it, and judges it, based on the symbolic co-related taught or learned intelligence that has been placed into the HDSA Dikw meta-cognition framework of bouton memory. All important and influential elements need to be first mentally selected and then co-related. Each causation identifies, symbolizes, and then co-relates the most relevant factors, in the final judgment for Self and others. One many is outside, the next inside, creating a much more complex calculation. That's the many-many body problem of consciousness.

Mbit, a new word, is a multi-bit used in calculating, in summing a/effect decision probabilities. A bit is an on/off switch placed into a relative memory position. A Qbit, a Quantum bit, is a bit that can have two values of differing probabilities. An Mbit is a bit that can have multiple polarities, one for each logic, with different probable values of affect and effect upon the framed decisions process. Boutons are not vectors or tensors. They are multivalued, probable, a/effectors; they are Mbits. As such, bouton Mbits quickly reach the many-many body problem and therefore require the strict limitation of variables in the decision-making calculations. Mbit factored inclusion, or not, is the first judgment of a Conscious brain/mind as it calculates situation meaning, decision, and action.

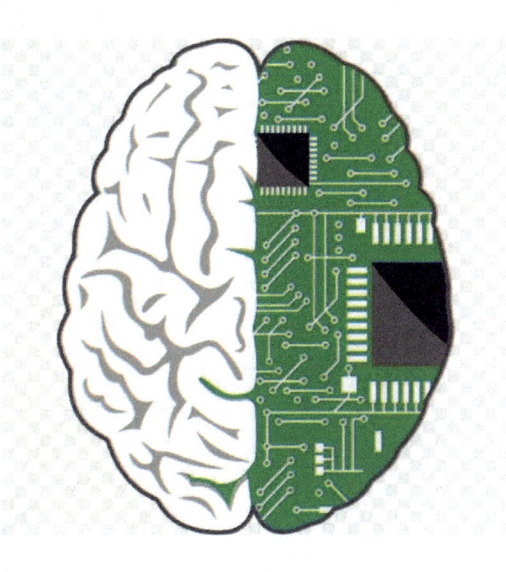

Meaning mapping is a statistical process of co-relating sensed forms (symbols), using the Mbits boutons of a multi-logically ordered combination, pointing onto a meaning and its resulting action.

Meme is a pattern of thought, culturally created and sustained throughout generations of humans. Memes are situation dependent and can be life providing or not. If this, and you want that, then act this way. A named meme defines that process symbolically. Linked memes makeup memory.

Memes are culturally selected situation/behavior instructions that build and decay the ideological structures in a CBM. They are culture defined, named situation-responses, carried as symbols upon electromagnetic waves. They are culturally determined ideas, linked into ideal quanta. They are decisions. The first meme is "Life more abundant". This is the first node in the taxonomy of Life.

Memory in humans is a remarkable substance. It has taken the Universe about 14 billion years, learning and advancing Life insights, from trial and error, to develop the memory of a Conscious brain/mind. Memory is a 4D, organic IPO computer of taught and feedback learned intentional symbols, that intentionally integrate creating intellect. From Afferent neuron input, to Cognitive neuron pathway decision-making (least energy rules), to Efferent gland and muscle output actions; memory remembers what works and does not work by intended (intents) situations (extents).

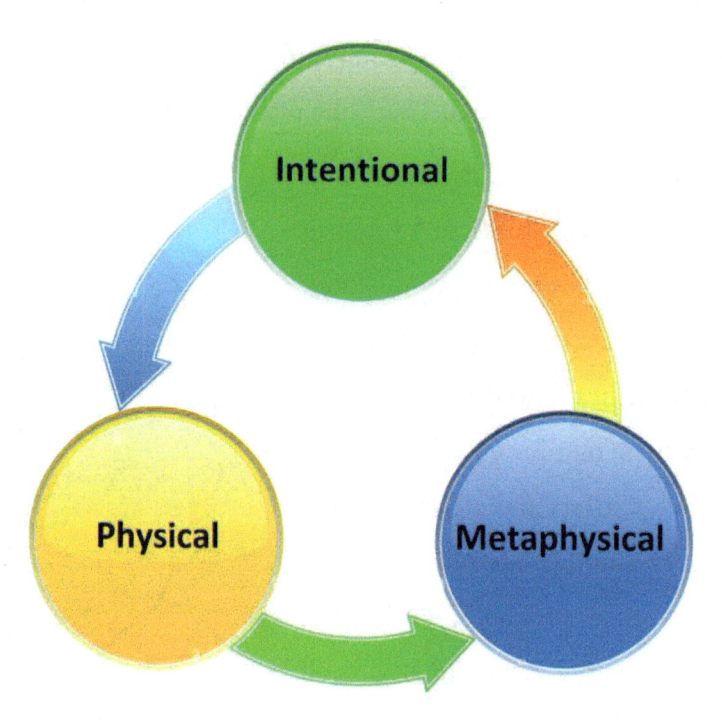

Meta is an ancient Greek word that means "beside". This is the form-symbols space above, below, before, and after the physical existence of the real thing now being discussed. There are both (1) physical and (2) metaphysical things found in formative spacetime. Both have intention. Each can be cross-modeled and function co-related more accurately using HDSA/Dikw symbolization.

Metacognition is a set of abstract ideas and methods that ideafold frame and define how symbols are intentionally processed in a Conscious brain/mind. This book introduces the HDSA/Dikw Partological method of thought. It is a metacognition. HDSA/Dikw skilled humans can become certified Metacognitions and use the CMC℠ (Certified Meta Cognition) service mark. Metacognition is the context of cognition. For example, an idea is a cog. Placing that idea into a mentally useful context is cognition. Metacognition is a more abstract thinking-tool (multi-logics) that you use to take cogs and place them into cognition; to improve intelligent life behaviors.

Metacognitions Society (www.Metacognitions.org) is a group of skilled Cognitive Scientists and Cognitive Engineer practitioners that will coordinate the cross-development, and sharing, of further Cognitive Scientific insights for humanity.

Mind boutons are presynaptic "buttons", are neurological growths that coordinate the firing of Action potential; from one neuron into another. Mind boutons grow, based on repetitive usage, in the synapse; connecting neuron paths. Bouton bits make up idea symbols that are then co-related intentionally. This coordination of bouton firings, based on electromagnetic symbols, is for Life.

Mind consciously senses, learns, and remembers how the physical world works. It intentionally remembers what works and does not work, by situation, for its more abundant lifetime. Mind is the co-related idea systems stored in boutons that fire or hold given the taught or learned situation. Boutons are the mind bits, the sub-parts of ideas, that make up and describe idealized situation behaviors. These boutons form symbol processing pathways that judge; using least energy rules.

Many-body is a name for understanding that real things a/effect other real things exponentially in 4D spacetime. Mathematically, many-body uses the body$^{\#}$ (body count to the <u>power</u> of body count and not bodies <u>times</u> bodies). All things change based on multiple factors. Each selected thing, judged to be materially a/effective upon the framed outcome, is a body that affects (future back) and effects (past forward) the outcome of those associated bodies. The association of relevant bodies collapse and connect, using partological methods, creating new bodily outcomes; a new materiality. The many-many-body problem of an a/effect analysis (two, a/e many-bodies to count). It is used to mathematically describes this added complexity. This is why judgment is probable.

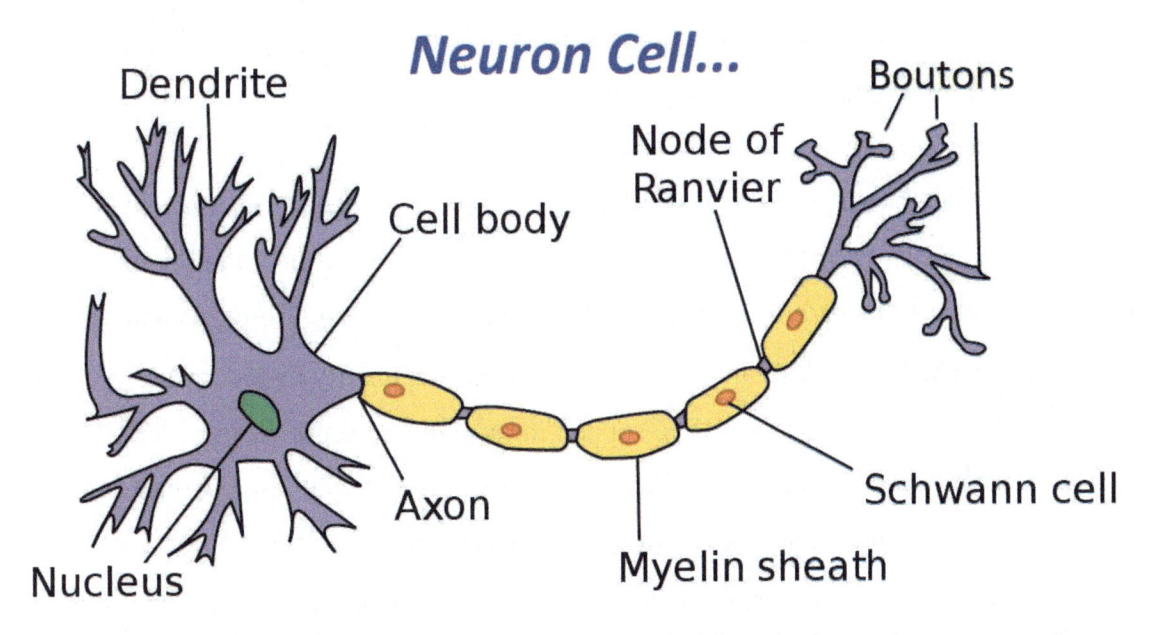

Neuron Cell...

Dendrite, Cell body, Axon, Nucleus, Node of Ranvier, Boutons, Schwann cell, Myelin sheath

Neurons are DNA created-and-placed cells that collect, hold, and release electromagnetic energy; into quantized standing or moving waves; collectively creating insightful symbols. Neurons are linked into a sense-in, decision-making, and instructions-out organic computer. Neuron dendrites (roots) accept electrical input from the upstream neurons. Axons (branches) move that energy to other neurons. The Action potential energy "jumps" via bouton (buds) in the synapse, transferring one bit of intellect. Bouton hold-or-fire pixelates conscious awareness.

Neuronal pathways, created by the linking of spacetime coordinated bouton firings, are built memories. A sensation, as content-in-context, is factored and directed by internal intent along a specific sense, decide, act neuronal pathway. This is a spiraled recursive process from Life-to-actions down and back-up to Life again. The Opportunity for Life more abundant is the probabilistic force, the most essential form, to individually and collectively formulate the past, current, and future Universe. Things want to get smart. They get smarter via neuronal pathways.

Objective symbols define and describe physical entities, outside the subject, in verbal relation to a subjective Self. They're part of subject/object/verb methods.

Opportunity-for-life (Op) is a future-back phenomenon. It starts in the future. It is not deduced or induced; but consciously conducted, point by point, via felt affection. Your conscious intentions change the opportunity for Life, for all.

Partology is an HDSA based thinking tool that orders Dikw symbols, creating a multi-logical conscious awareness of Self, in various situations. It understands, names, and HDSA/Dikw maps how, where, when, who, and why named parts go into and out of desired wholes. Partology is the multilogical part-to-whole engineering method, derived from Cognitive Science. It mathematically symbolizes how parts go into, and out of, wholes; the quanta steps. It, that formalization, formulates wisdom and knowledge from data and information.

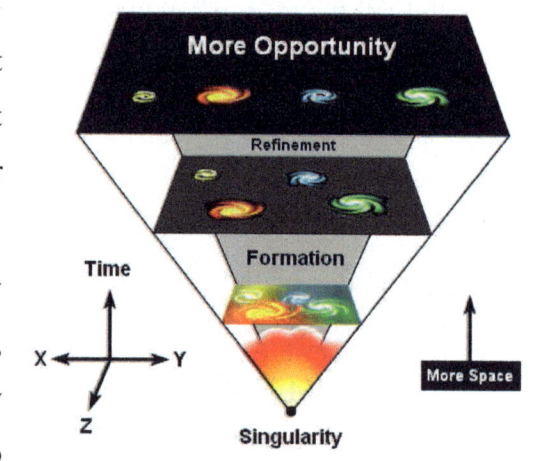

Partology/HDSA/Dikw symbols are intention structured and directly linked, recursive containers for thought. Partology creates a set of co-related ideas about creating clearer ideas. It creates a known and useful metacognition. It's how content-in-context cognition works intentionally overlapping multiple, simultaneous symbolic logics. Cogs, those situation boutons, wheel on.

Peripheral Nervous System (PNS) contains two sets of connected neurons: (1) the Afferent neurons capture and transfer sensation symbol input into the Cognitive neurons in the cranium and (2) the Efferent neurons receive and transfer instruction output to glands, cells, and muscles.

Pointing out the relevant factors that affect an outcome (in thinking, composing, and doing) occurs point-by-point; with each point being thought about in context of all other relevant points. Each

82 Your Conscious brain/mind

point is developed inside-out and placed outside-in. This is a recursive process of symbols kept to a minimum. Pointing out the relevant a/effective parts create a tersely integrated Partology; that situation ideology. Simply, know and remember how parts go into and out of intended wholes.

Prove ascertains: Any new theory starts with defining the terms. Then it logically co-relates these terms in spacetime, into a provable or unprovable theoretical ascertain, that can be materially tested. We prove the HDSA/Dikw Partology theory, by making people smarter.

Quantum is a thought-tool (first used by Planck) that physically, logically, and mathematically co-relates the intentional and extensional factors of a defined situation; statistically causing a measured change. A quantum is a bouton. A bouton is a quantum. Quantum mechanics mathematically defines how both physical and ideological quanta a/affect each other. "Conscious mechanics" is to idea stored memory memes what Quantum mechanics is to physical parts.

Quantum mechanics is a formal mathematics, the best yet developed, for understanding and modeling physical change. It states that parts wave; parts are waves, they wave into and out of being. Quantum mechanics advances Classical mechanics but is incomplete (says Einstein, Schrödinger, and Dirac). Conscious mechanics is more complete because it takes "Self" conscious awareness and intent, those metaphysical forces, into the physical equations of Life more abundant. The electromagnetic overlapping waves, both standing and moving, do not directionally collapse until strongly intended; either internally or externally and maybe both in alignment. Observational intent is needed, collapsing the probable waves, to make the world go forward.

Opportunity for Life is materially created in, and by, material in spacetime. Life opportunity is a Universe created factor that generationally fulfills itself anew. Life learns to live better, for longer, on less. Each advancing stage is an ideological and formative new life form. It's an evolved quantum of Life; symbolically uncovered and physically made anew.

Recuring context, not in a homogeneous continuing field but in a situation varying frame (an ideafold), is how the World is and how the Conscious brain/mind uses memory to make short- and long-term life decisions. This ideological "framed terrain" pre-exists in memory before each CBM contextual decision and action affects the new probable intelligence stored in that intentionally framed ideafold. Mechanically this is achieved with one adaptive algorithm that first "selects and sets" the frame before the "thinking" occurs; resulting in a decision to then act, observe, and remember. No "situation-action" is also remembered and stored in the ideafold as not acted upon.

Self, the so-called "hard problem" of consciousness, is your overall one point, as created and supported by the related memory subpoints. The symbolic form of the Self is self-selected for life. You make up your Self for good or ill. Self is a metaphysical, ideological structure that influences bouton bits and their intentionally aligned neurological pathways of behavior. All individuals have a unique Self. That Self can be consciously idealized. It's a plan before it's physically developed. The Self is stored in, and understood by, the personal behaviors; your habits.

Self-organization principles (agencies) are invariant under mental and physical transformations. Life intends the same, is unchanged, regardless of the then current bouton co-relations. Life is for more life. HDSA multi-logics is a Dikw symbolized, Self-organizing structure because each level has a higher, more desired and essential Life point.

Seriality is a logical method consisting of, forming part of, and taking place in a set of one-dimensional steps. A procedure or work instruction uses serial logic to explain the intentions; at and onto a point. Serial logic is the "S" in HDSA multi-logics.

Smart knows what to do when; selecting and manifesting an internal intent; smart is for Life. Smart people live better, for longer, on less. They are Life smart. Plus, they are civil. Dumb people are less smart and less civilized. They live less and die early. In fact, evil people are already dead.

Spacetime does not contain consciousness. It is too limited. It, the spacetime term, was created by conscious awareness. Instead, consciousness comes from pre-spacetime agency and is mediated into the intentional-material spacetime. Conscious awareness sees matter (1) as it exists and (2) as it can be anew in space over time. Alternative selections are Self intentional.

Subjective symbols, semantically and syntactically supported by objects and verbs, define and describe ideologies; as they intentionally select bouton pathways, creating, and maintaining a Self.

Symbol is a formative representation of physical reality. They are carried upon the co-relations of Electromagnetic energy waves. Co-related symbols collapse into, and radiate from, material particles based on the collective, and relative, affective intents. Schrödinger's cat probably lives-or-dies by the co-relationship of the intentional symbolic forms; as physical instantiated. Conscious behavior is related from and onto these symbolic formations.

Teleonomy is a pre-formed method of goal-directed behavior caused by both the physical structure, ideological intentions, and the naturally extending Life functions of all living organisms. Each structure has function, that is causal, and so it goes. Particles wave, buttons open or close.

Terms are ideas. Any new theory starts with defining the terms. Then it logically co-relates these terms in spacetime to provide provable and/or unprovable theoretical ascertains; that can be materially tested. A Scientific theory is a set of terms, supported by a math, that can be tested.

Tesimal numbering is a Combinatorial math method that measures relative hierarchy, dimensionality, seriality, with alternatives; at the same time, using the one number. Tesimal numbers are not imaginary; they are real. Think of Tesimal numbering as a "Tree" numbering system that precisely represents the co-related HDSA multi-logical points; describing reality.

Three layers refers to the brain, mind, and conscious awareness. A Conscious brain/mind (CBM) intentionally integrates these layers. This layering is an on-point, recursive, spirally intentional action. Accurate consciousness looks down, up, out, and in before it decides for Life.

Truth (as both a current statement and future prediction) is a real, idea symbolization, that is judged ideal. Truth is probable. All three layers multi-bodily a/effect the "true statement" prediction percent, at the same time. Life is most true.

Uncertainty always exists. Each thing affects (pulls) and effects (pushes) all other things. In addition, conscious things change their intentions and actions as they will. These willful idea changes create the new, future formations. In this uncertainty is found the opportunity for Life more abundant; for us all.

> Do as you will
> Will as done...

Universe is all there is and will be. It is the idea for all space, time, matter, information, formations, and willful intention; now, next, and forever. It's the one verse. Essentially, the Universe is for Life advancing. The Universe today, its available matter, is being constantly reformed by the co-relations of the collective conscious intention of all living things. Intellect control materiality.

Verbs symbol define and describe material or thinking causes. Verbs nomenclate the assembly or decay "actions" between and by intentional subjects (Self) and extensional objects (matter).

Wisdom, the W part of Dikw, is knowing when to apply what know-how. It is always a judgment before an action. Wisdom can insightfully and productively better manage those important things, for your lifetime. It is wise to be moral because Life-aligned groups are more powerful.

You will get it bit-by-bit. That's how the advanced Conscious brain/mind is developed. Just start it by knowing what to intend for Life. Make essential choices first. Then add the supportive parts.

You Program You (YPY). It is important to note that Cognitive scientific insight does <u>not</u> program you. Cognitive Science only describes how the Conscious brain/mind works in human beings. You, the Self, the specific individual, selects what to think, do, and be. YPY. Cognitive Science multi-logically describes how to do that. This metacognition insight helps you do that.

What do all of these terms really say? **Think better!** Be more precise and organized in your mentally framed lifetime. Set the frame. Identified the Dikw elements. Co-relate the a/effects in HDSA space over time. Make the decision and observe the results. Learn from that. In short, consciously learn to live better each day. Do this for all of us. That is the road up.

Clear observation, your good intention to explore and understand, a/effects both physical and metaphysical beings. So, get better at paying attention to what really matters; both short and long term. This is HDSA/Dikw multi-logical way up.

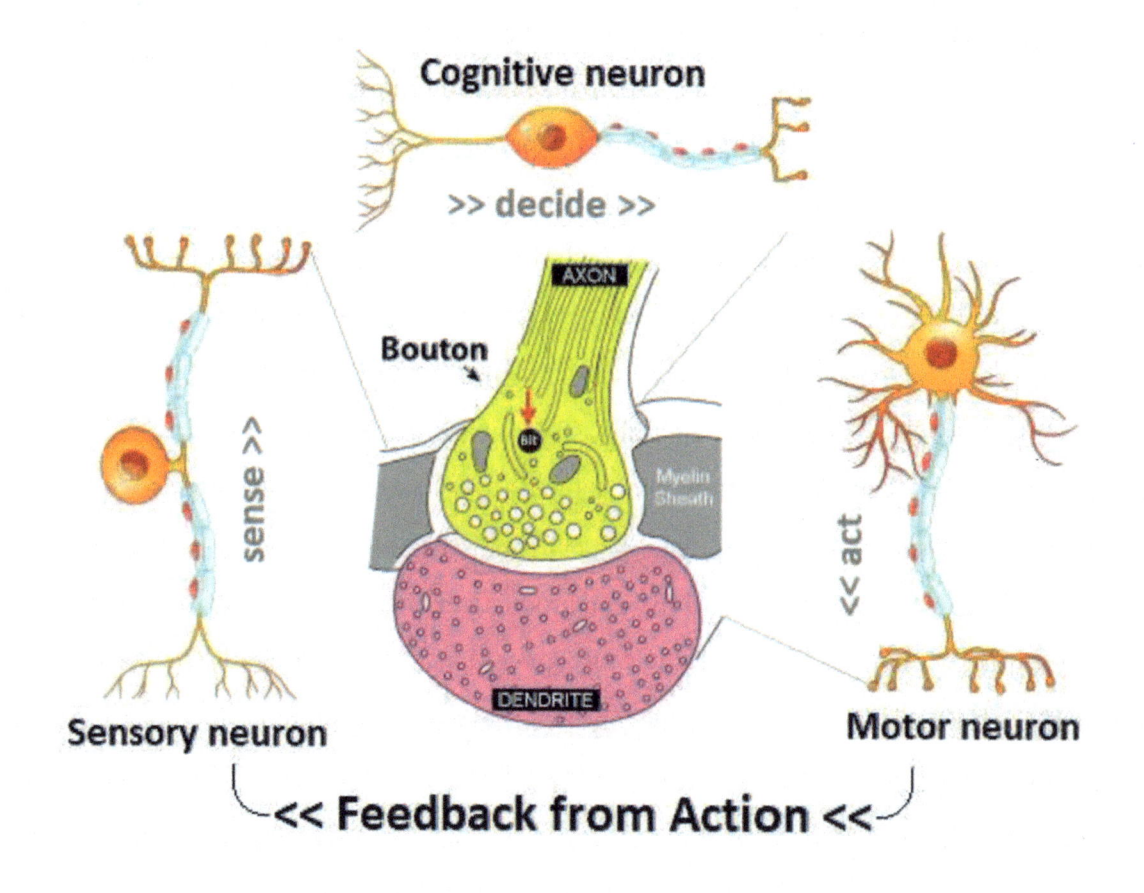

The Moral Part of Cognitive Science

Cognitive Science studies reason, intuition, and morality because these three connect mutually, affecting the quality of Life. A student once said, "I don't understand the connection between HDSA/Dikw multi-logics and morality. How does making me more logical also make me more moral?" Let's discuss this a bit.

We start with Life; for you, me, and us all. Cognitive Science is a Life Science. The point of reason, intuition, and moral behaviors are to create a better lifetime for us all, individually and in groups. Life is not a Zero-sum game. Instead, it is creative. More Life can be created for all.

Morality directly affects life quality. Both reason and intuition are affected by your moral codes. Your moral and just being influences how smart you can become.

In the Conscious brain/mind there is a cross-symbiotic relationship between reason, intuition, and moral behaviors. They are three different points of view, that overlap, all causing better lifetimes.

For example, lying makes you stupid. Systemic lying makes you evil. This is because lies get bouton instantiated, creating ideological disharmony in a Conscious brain/mind. In a liar, their Conscious brain/mind develops many incorrect conduits of thought that work at cross purposes. The lie is mentally remembered as a rational scar. This is the basis of "O what an evil web you weave when first you practice to deceive."

So, this Cognitive Scientist suggests that you do not lie. Instead, learn to tell the truth well. You can appropriately say the truth for your audience and objective. Say it so they "get it" and get value from it. Say it so you also get value from it. Those sayings add to the life of us all.

Promoting truth-telling is one way that HDSA/Dikw Partology improves the moral fiber of people. There is another logical factor at work that causes moral behavior to be chosen, promoted, and lived.

Selfish behavior is not always good. Otherish behavior, giving more than you get, is also skewed. We'ish behavior, promoting the benefit for all, is the moral sweet-spot rationally taught in Cognitive Science. All people involved can "Have their cake and eat it too". You just must think-it-out that way. Together, we are always better. That is the moral sweet-spot.

What is **We'ism**? It's an understanding, a point of view, and behavior action that thinks about and fosters group synergies. Ask yourself, how can all people properly participate and get fairly rewarded? Who makes up that team? We'ism promotes the efficient and successful behaviors of both individuals and their selected groups. It's a we'istic point of view that is supported by the most useful, Life advancing behaviors.

Think about this we'istic cognitive method a bit. Is Life a "Zero Sum" game? Is there only so much life to go around that must be divided up? The answer is no. Life is elastic; it is created anew each day by more intelligent group behaviors. Consciousness creates life or death results because it reforms matter. More life can be created, with the same matter, by the individual and their group.

In short, people that can work together are more productive. They live better, for longer, on less. Why? It is easier, more fun, and more intelligent to master-mind the solution for all people involved; as appropriate.

Again, do not be selfish or otherish. Instead, look for the group synergies that create more for less for all. Know and be your productive role in that synergistic group. That is the we'ish way forward for Life more abundant, for one and all.

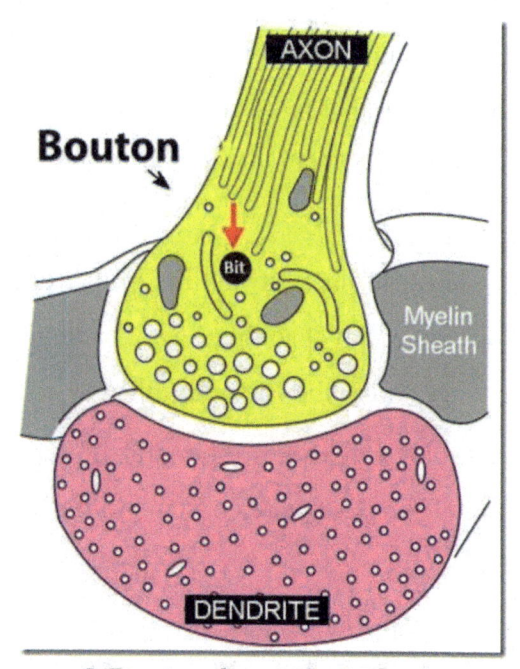

A Bouton is a Mind Pixel.

Boutons live better in coordinated groups. Isolated, not used boutons kill their neuron. No bouton is an island. Instead, they co-relate for the improved quality of their lifetime. Both the symbols, and the symbolic pathways from sensation, cognition, and action, are based on the intended-for-life insights and behaviors of coordinated boutons. Not used boutons kill neurons.

When a bouton joins a recuring reasoned-collective; they live better, for longer, on less. This happens because they get fed neuronal "Action potential" more often than not. Use it or lose it. Being part of a collective allows you to use it more often.

88 Your Conscious brain/mind

Cognitive Science teaches us how our Conscious brain/mind works; it defines Conscious mechanics.

The goal is to get smarter. This means we each can learn to live better, for longer, on less. Bit-by-bit, connected symbol by connected symbol, the insightful HDSA Dikw herein will help you do just that.

The World is complex. It is getting more difficult and more competitive every day. If you know how the World works, both physically and psychologically, you can take direct mental action to make it work better for you and us all. As you improve your situation-specific mindsets (that set of ideas, now right for you), you become healthier, better looking, better dressed, improve friendships, make more money per hour worked, are happier, can afford to buy a nice house, save money, etc. The smarter you are, the better your life. Intelligence is the recipe for lifelong success.

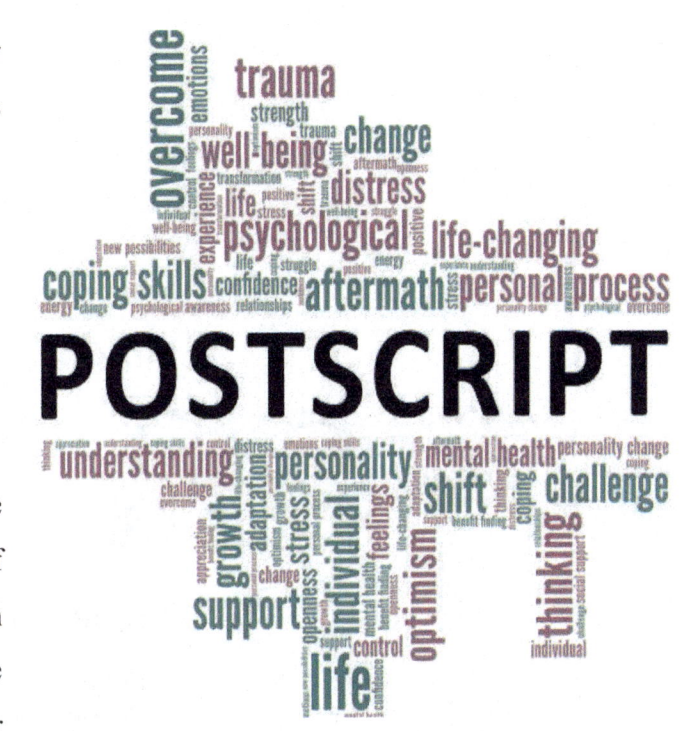

To do this, to get smarter, you must know about your Conscious brain/mind. You must know how it works to make it work better. What is the brain? What is mind? What is consciousness? Why is each Dikw symbolized part linked using HDSA multi-logics? How does an HDSA/Dikw multi-logical structure model my current intentions?

All of this is called Partology. It is the essence of Cognitive Science. It is how cogs understand, model, and create the future. If you use the "HDSA/Dikw Partological" thought-tool, that metacognition, to think about and act out, then your thoughts will be more efficient. Less can then get more. We all live better. That is the overall point.

"Faith in the future, out of the now." ~ John Lennon, Mind Games

Thank you all...

As I began to think about whom to thank, in the writing of this book, the number of named people who have helped me approaches 1,000. I am a product of my family, upbringing, education, experience, work effort, relationships, cities I've lived in, culture, etc.

We all are; all humans come from other people. That's what makes us so unique. That combination of past ideas and future creativity, is a lot of stuff.

So, who do I thank?

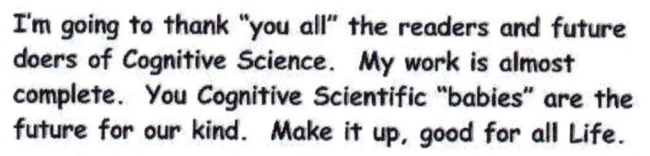

I'm going to thank "you all" the readers and future doers of Cognitive Science. My work is almost complete. You Cognitive Scientific "babies" are the future for our kind. Make it up, good for all Life.

I thank you all. -g

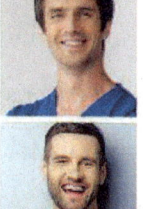

90 Your Conscious brain/mind

About the Author

I have been doing this for a long time. In 1971-1972, I spent my Cornell University junior year abroad in England studying "Commodity Buying Behavior in the European Economic Community". There, in an Economics course entitled "Resource Allocation and Control," the professors introduced the idea of a new science called "Cognitive Science"; coming from three professors at Edinburgh University in Scotland.

This fit me. My dad, William John Deines, started with IBM in 1955. As Cub Scouts, we were taken to see the IBM 1401 punch card "data processing machines" operating at the State House in Topeka, Kansas. As an Explorer Scout, we were back to see the first Kansas IBM 360 Mainframe at work, creating Management Information (MIS). I initially got digital bits in my blood.

However, the son must always do better than dad. My dad had already done computers. So, in my lifetime, I would understand how the bio-computer worked. That started at Cornell, a 50-year research project culminating in the useful metacognitive ideas in this book.

Along the way, Cajal introduced me to "boutons" with his 1906 Nobel Prize in medicine (shared with Golgi). Then Eccles spoke of Consciousness being a Quantum mechanical process; in a 1961 paper. With the bouton bit and the quantum nature of consciousness, I got my foothold.

A few innovative ideas emerged that were needed to take the next steps. For example, a bouton is a mind bit (Mbit). The Conscious brain/mind is physical, symbolic, and intention; all at the same time. Life supersedes conscious awareness, and life "Opportunity" is logically and intuitively "conducted" into a CBM. Good ideas appear creatively. Finally, the a/effect force and the Deinian math that represents these "causations", not equations, needed the Tesimal numbering schema.

Each of these linked ideas helped me logically and mathematically define "Conscious mechanics" and uncover how the Conscious brain/mind works. In this book, I have tried to simplify the process with HDSA/Dikw Partology. That multi-logical way of thinking, this symbolic partological framework, will make you smarter. It is a Universal.

In this new mental frame, this new metacognition, the better ideas themselves will intentionally align. It is really as simple as that. -- Gary Deines, Cognitive Scientists, Nahant, MA, USA

This is the back cover…

Metacognition Certification #YYMMDD543

THIS ACKNOWLEDGES THAT

Recipient Name

HAS SUCCESSFULLY COMPLETED THE

Cognitive Science Course and Personal Coursework
and is licensed to use CMC℠ as a Certified Metacognition.

Month, Day, Year   *Gary Deines, President*

BOUTONICS

To all Metacognitions…

The purpose of this book is to teach how the Conscious brain/mind works. Once a person understands (1) brain neurons, (2) mind boutons and (3) the metaphysical nature of intentional self-awareness; that person can then take direct symbolic action to get smarter. They will use HDSA formatted multi-logics, of explicit Dikw symbolism (meme content in context), to ideologically program themself anew. They then get smarter.

Those people live better, for longer, on less. Plus, they are more civil; are better team players.

A few will then want to become [Metacognitions](). These are people who commercially teach and train HDSA/Dikw multi-logics to others. They attend the www.CogSci101.com course of study (provided from many locations), conduct and complete their personalized casework, pass the exam, and then apply for Metacognitions certification.

These certified experts may apply to the "Metacognitions Society" (www.Metacognitions.org), gain membership, and will coordinate the cross-development, and sharing, of further Cognitive Scientific insights for humanity.

Certified Metacognitions, in good standing, are authorized to display and use the CMC Service Mark (Certified Meta Cognition) in their career work and/or business entity marketing.

We can improve the world.

Made in the USA
Columbia, SC
17 August 2023